Football School

Name: ....

Class: ....

Coaches: ....

Kickito Ergo Sum

To Josh, star (keyboard) player – A.B.

To ABC, and M, with love – B.L.

For Lizzie, my inspirational and intrepid niece – S.G.

First published 2019 by Walker Books Ltd
87 Vauxhall Walk, London SE11 5HJ

8 10 9

This book has been typeset in Palatino

Printed and bound by CPI Group (UK) Ltd, Croydon CR0 4YY

British Library Cataloguing in Publication Data:
a catalogue record for this book is available from the British Library

ISBN 978-1-4063-8641-7

WALKER BOOKS

FSC www.fsc.org MIX Paper from responsible sources FSC® C020471

www.walker.co.uk

www.footballschool.co

FOOTBALL SCHOOL

STAR PLAYERS

50

INSPIRING STORIES OF TRUE FOOTBALL HEROES

ALEX BELLOS & BEN LYTTLETON

Illustrated by Spike Gerrell

Welcome to Football School Star Players!
Nice to see you again! I'm Alex.
And I'm Ben. We're your coaches.
We can't wait to tell you about our fifty all-time favourite footballers.
We think our Star Players are the greatest! Not only are they all brilliant with the ball, but they are also inspirational off the pitch too.
We've chosen fearsome defenders, magical midfielders, high-scoring forwards and the canniest coaches in the history of the game.
We've also selected players who have made an incredible impact on the world. You'll discover:
The African centre-forward who became president of his country.
He gets our vote!
The World Cup winner donating her brain to science.
She's using her head!

The midfielder who invented a football boot that changed the game.
Boot-iful!
The Dutchman who inspired a tactical revolution.
TOTALLY!
You'll learn about the top stars playing today, and also some amazing characters from decades ago.
They're listed in alphabetical order, and we have awarded them badges based on their achievements: SCORER for the goal-getters, STOPPER for keepers and sweepers, INNOVATOR for creative players and trailblazers and LEADER for captains and coaches.
At the end of the book there's a quiz. So pay attention!
Otherwise it could get very Messi.
Don't Bale out on us now.
Are you ready? It all starts in a Mo!

FOOTBALL SCHOOL

STAR COACH

ALEX

Country: England
Major clubs: Chess club, reading club, nightclub
Position: Sitting at a desk
International highlights: Travelling down a river in the Amazon rainforest in a small boat
Individual awards: School Christmas Card Competition winner aged 8

STAR STAT

About 70,000 curly hairs on his head

Key | = reader | haha! = joker | = worrier | = adder

MEET YOUR COACHES

STAR COACH

BEN

Country: England

Major clubs: Table tennis club, poetry club, Club biscuits

Position: Running with my dog

International highlights: Learning some Hungarian to interview Ferenc Puskás in his homeland

Individual awards: Best penalty-taker in school Under-11 team

STAR STAT

8 toppings on his favourite pizza

Key | = writer | ZZZ = sleeper | = runner | = eater

CONTENTS

STAR PLAYER

ENIOLA ALUKO

Fearless forward and lawyer who stands up for her rights

STAR STAT

102

appearances for England

Born: 1987
Country: England
Position: Forward
Major clubs: Chelsea (England), Juventus (Italy)
International highlights: Finalist, 2009 Euros; semi-finalist, 2015 World Cup

Key | = leader | = innovator | = scorer | = stopper

Eniola Aluko is unafraid to speak up, both on and off the pitch. She is one of England's most successful women footballers, as well as a respected pundit and lawyer. She has also shown great courage in standing up against discrimination.

Born in Nigeria, Aluko moved to England when she was a baby. As a child, she played football in local parks with her younger brother, Sone, who would go on to play as a forward in the Premier League. Sone said that his sister gave him the confidence to become a professional.

Aluko was always heading for the top. She made her England debut aged seventeen and went on to play 102 times and score 33 goals for England. She won two league titles with Chelsea before she moved to Italy to play for Juventus. She also lifted the FA Cup trophy with three different teams (Charlton, Birmingham and Chelsea) and played in the England team that reached the 2009 European Championship final and the 2015 World Cup semi-final.

Her football achievements are only part of her incredible story. Aluko's father was a politician, and a passion for justice runs in her family. After she read *To Kill a Mockingbird* at school, a novel about a man accused of a crime he didn't commit, she was determined to become a lawyer. "I liked the idea of having a voice for the voiceless, getting someone justice against the odds," she said.

While playing for England, Aluko studied for a law degree. She specialised in contract law and has negotiated on behalf of huge stars to get them the best deal possible. Her impressive list of clients included former England captain David Beckham and Belgium's World Cup hero Eden Hazard.

She was also the first woman to appear as a pundit on BBC's *Match of the Day*, where her analysis of matches was highly respected. In 2018, she became one of the first women to commentate on the men's World Cup. Her impressive tactical breakdown of the teams won her admiration from everyone.

> "STANDING UP FOR WHAT YOU BELIEVE IN IS LIBERATING."
> Eniola Aluko

Aluko has always been prepared to use her voice off the pitch. When the England coach made racist comments to her and another player, Aluko publicly spoke out against him. She lost her place in the team and was ignored by some of her team-mates. But after numerous investigations, she was proved to have been telling the truth.

Aluko has also used her high profile to ask that football clubs offer young female players the same educational opportunities that male players are given. "My issue is young, talented players not having to compromise their education," she said. She also thinks the salaries of female players should be increased so they are closer to what male players earn.

Aluko is a champion of equality, who has inspired others to stand up for their rights, even in the face of adversity – just like the hero of her favourite book.

STAR PLAYER

ROBERTO BAGGIO

Best player in the world who missed a penalty in the World Cup final

Born: 1967
Country: Italy
Position: Forward
Major clubs: Fiorentina, Juventus, AC Milan, Inter Milan (all Italy)
International highlights: Semi-finalist, 1990 World Cup; finalist, 1994 World Cup
Individual awards: Winner, 1993 Ballon D'Or

STAR STAT

108
penalties scored in his career

Key | = leader | = innovator | = scorer | = stopper

Six months after he won the Ballon D'Or award for the world's best player, Roberto Baggio missed a penalty kick for Italy in the 1994 World Cup final – and so handed the trophy to Brazil. Imagine scoring over 200 amazing goals and only being remembered for the one you missed!

That is typical of Baggio's complicated football career. He played in the number ten position, just behind the centre-forward, and he was as comfortable creating goals as scoring them. He had the vision to craft a pass or shot out of nothing, and could find space with an effortless elegance. But it wasn't always easy for him and he never won as many trophies as his talent deserved.

He first came to prominence as a teenager at Vicenza but, two days before he was due to complete a move to Fiorentina, he injured his knee. The move still went ahead and over the next five years, Baggio was feted as one of the club's best ever players. In 1990, he left Fiorentina because Juventus offered £8 million, a world-record fee at the time.

He was still at Juventus when the 1994 World Cup came around. By now, Baggio had been voted the world's best and he was Italy's key player. He scored both goals in the 2–1 win against Nigeria in the round of 16, and the winning goal against Spain in the quarter-final. He scored two more against Bulgaria in the semi-final. But he hobbled off with 20 minutes left, clutching his hamstring. The final, against Brazil, was four days later: would he be fit?

No one knew if Baggio would play. On the morning of the game, Baggio told Italy coach Arrigo Sacchi that he wanted to play – even though he was not fully fit. The Italy coach picked him because his goals had helped Italy reach the final. It was a way of thanking him for his previous performances. Italy, who had won three World Cups before, was one match away from winning a fourth. Baggio missed two chances in the final, and later said that he thought he would have scored if he had been fully fit.

The game ended 0–0 and was the first World Cup final to go to a penalty shoot-out. Two Italy players missed, so by the time Baggio stepped up, he needed to score to keep Italy in the game. He was usually excellent at taking penalties – his scoring record from the spot was an impressive 86 per cent – but remember, he was not at his best. Baggio aimed down the middle of the goal but the ball sailed three metres over the crossbar. Brazil had won – or rather, Italy (and Baggio) had lost – the World Cup.

Only five players have missed a penalty in a World Cup final penalty shoot-out:

NAME	NATIONAL TEAM	MATCH
Franco Baresi	Italy	1994 World Cup final
Márcio Santos	Brazil	1994 World Cup final
Daniele Massaro	Italy	1994 World Cup final
Roberto Baggio	Italy	1994 World Cup final
David Trézéguet	France	2006 World Cup final

No one blamed Baggio for missing – even if he admitted the moment gave him nightmares for a long time after. He had converted to Buddhism early in his career, and said the religion helped him find inner peace. He continued to take, and score, penalties and, after his World Cup disaster, he helped Juventus and then AC Milan win the Italian championship, the only two league titles of his career.

Baggio's story shows that everyone can make mistakes, and even the greatest of players have to confront failure. Baggio stayed calm, focused on his game and bounced back. For him, being happy – and helping others – was the most important thing! As for Italy, their next World Cup final appearance, in 2006, ended in another penalty shoot-out: and this time, they won!

STAR PLAYER

GARETH BALE

Welsh wizard with a habit of scoring in Champions League finals

STAR STAT

€100 MILLION transfer fee paid by Real Madrid

Born: 1989
Country: Wales
Position: Winger
Major clubs: Tottenham Hotspur (England), Real Madrid (Spain)
International highlights: Semi-finalist, 2016 Euros

Key | = leader | = innovator | = scorer | = stopper

Gareth Bale became the most expensive player in history when Real Madrid bought him from Spurs for €100 million in 2013. But he was worth the money! The Welsh wizard has won four Champions League finals at Madrid, scoring decisive goals in three of them, including one of the most dazzling goals in the history of the tournament.

Bale grew up in Cardiff and was spotted as a nine-year-old by Southampton, who invited him to train at their youth academy. But he was a skinny teenager, and the club almost didn't give him a contract because they thought he wasn't strong enough. However, he had a brilliant left foot and could beat almost every opponent for speed. He was called up to play for his country, Wales, almost immediately and became their youngest player (at sixteen) and scorer (at seventeen). Although eligible to play for England (as he has an English grandmother), Bale has always been a proud Welshman and sees it as an honour to represent his country.

After success at Southampton, Bale moved to Tottenham Hotspur. But an ankle injury almost ended his career and he didn't win a Premier League game in his first 24 appearances for Spurs – one coach claimed that he was jinxed. But he kept working hard and became the most important player in the Spurs team, creating and scoring goals out of nothing. He also took a mean free kick!

After he scored 26 goals for Spurs in one season, Real Madrid signed him for a record-breaking fee. In Spain, Bale missed his favourite chicken restaurant (as well as teabags and British chocolate) and did not find it easy to learn Spanish. But he remained calm and focused on his strengths: his pace and his left foot, which has always been a lethal weapon for crossing and shooting.

Bale has made a habit of scoring in big games for Real Madrid, including a solo goal in the 2014 Copa del Rey final against Barcelona, and a header in the 2014 Champions League final against Atlético Madrid. He started the 2018 Champions League final against Liverpool as a substitute. Bale came off the bench at 1–1 and almost immediately launched into an overhead kick that flew into the top of the net – among the best goals ever scored in a final! He followed that with a 30-yard shot that flew in. What a super-sub!

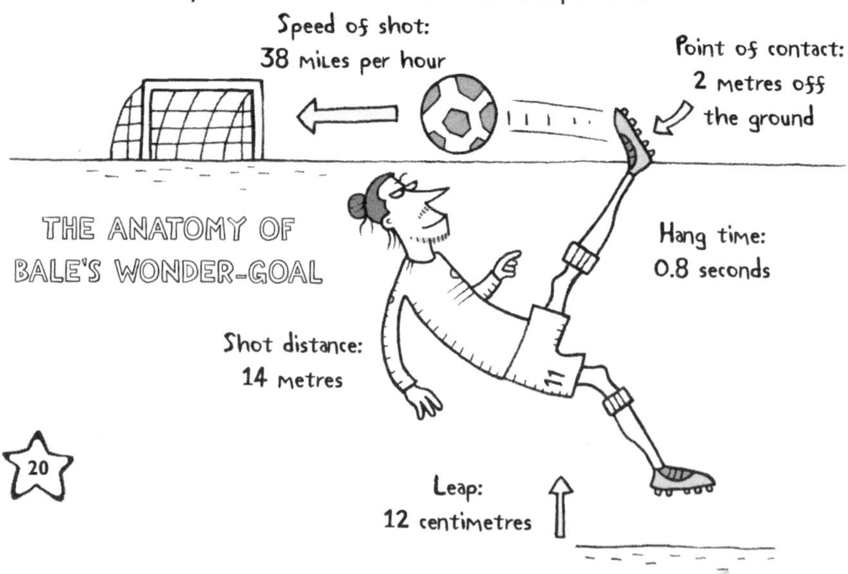

Despite being one of Real Madrid's biggest stars, Bale never forgets his homeland. He draped himself in a Wales flag after Real Madrid's first Champions League win. When Wales qualified for the 2016 Euros, their first international tournament for nearly 50 years, Bale scored six and assisted two of Wales's nine goals. He scored three more goals in the tournament – including a free kick against England – as Wales reached the semi-final. Bale said it was one of the proudest moments of his career.

Bale's career has been shaped by his perseverance, resilience, humility and a strong work ethic – through both the good times and bad. He has an unwavering belief in his own ability and knows that he can make an impact in matches if the coach picks him. "One man cannot make a team," said one reporter who covers Welsh football. "But he can make a team believe."

> "I DON'T FEEL I'VE CHANGED AT ALL, EVEN FROM THE UNDER-NINES. I DON'T THINK I EVER WILL."
>
> Gareth Bale

STAR PLAYER

FRANZ BECKENBAUER

Captain and coach who mastered a new role for defenders

Born: 1945
Country: Germany
Position: Defender
Major clubs: Bayern Munich (Germany)
International highlights (as player): Winner, 1972 Euros; winner, 1974 World Cup; finalist, 1976 Euros
International highlights (as coach): Winner, 1990 World Cup
Individual awards: Winner, 1972 and 1976 Ballon D'Or

STAR STAT

2
World Cups won

Key | = leader | = innovator | = scorer | = stopper

Tall, commanding and elegant, Franz Beckenbauer was the first man to lift the World Cup as captain and then coach. He also mastered a new role on the pitch: the sweeper, playing as the furthest defender back (and therefore sweeping up the ball).

> "BECKENBAUER WAS ONE OF THE BEST I EVER SAW PLAY."
>
> Pelé

Beckenbauer joined his local club, Bayern Munich, as a fourteen-year-old midfielder. He gradually moved into defence and helped turn Bayern from a newly promoted, unfashionable team to Bundesliga champions and three-time winners of the European Cup (the forerunner to the Champions League). Beckenbauer was an innovator who put an attacking spin on the sweeper position. He often ran into the opposition half to start attacks or even take shots himself. As no one had thought to mark the sweeper, he had space and time to cause havoc.

Beckenbauer, known as *Der Kaiser,* or The Emperor, also shone on the international stage. West Germany won the 1972 Euros and, in the same year, Beckenbauer became the first defender in history to win the Ballon D'Or. He was outstanding when West Germany won the 1974 World Cup, beating his rival Johan Cruyff's Netherlands 2–1 in the final.

Beckenbauer then coached the national team to success at the 1990 World Cup final, and his charisma, authority and composure came to represent the heart of German football. To this day, he remains one of the greatest defenders to have played the game.

STAR PLAYER

DAVID BECKHAM

Hard-working England captain who became a global celebrity

Born: 1975
Country: England
Position: Midfielder
Major clubs: Manchester United (England), Real Madrid (Spain), AC Milan (Italy), LA Galaxy (USA), Paris Saint-Germain (France)
International highlights: Scored in 1998, 2002 and 2006 World Cup; played in 2000 Euros

STAR STAT

Scored in
3
World
Cups

Key | = leader | = innovator | = scorer | = stopper

David Beckham was a free-kick specialist who fulfilled his dream of captaining England. He was also an underwear model who married a pop star and became one of the most famous people in the world. No other player has combined so successfully the worlds of football and celebrity.

Beckham was born in London but always supported Manchester United, who signed him aged sixteen. He was part of the Class of '92, the United youth team that won the 1992 FA Youth Cup, along with Ryan Giggs, Gary Neville and Paul Scholes. They would all go on to make history for United by forming the spine of the team during the club's most successful period.

Beckham won his first Premier League trophy in 1996. But it was only on the first day of the following season, when he scored a wonder goal against Wimbledon from inside his own half, that he became a superstar. Suddenly, everyone in England knew who he was. Not long after, he married a member of the Spice Girls, one of the world's biggest pop bands, and he became known all over the world.

Beckham continued to work hard to improve his game, practising his free-kick technique every day. His crosses from the wing, whipped in with curl and accuracy, were almost impossible to defend. Any corner kick or free kick was a goal-scoring opportunity with Beckham around. With his Predator boots, he was expert at swerving the ball around walls and past goalkeepers.

He scored from a free kick in the 1998 World Cup against Colombia, just a few days before one of the toughest moments of his career. In a crucial knock-out game against Argentina, Beckham kicked out at Argentina defender Diego Simeone and was sent off. England lost the game on penalties and Beckham was blamed for the defeat. He was deeply apologetic and eventually won back the fans' support in 2001. By then he was wearing the captain's armband and he scored the free-kick goal against Greece which qualified England for the 2002 World Cup. Beckham had become a hero again and his redemption was complete. He had shown remarkable resilience in the face of this adversity.

CAPTAIN FANTASTIC

Only three players have captained England more times than David Beckham. Here are the top five:

PLAYER	GAMES AS CAPTAIN	TOTAL GAMES	ENGLAND CAREER
Billy Wright	90	105	1946–1959
Bobby Moore	90	108	1962–1973
Bryan Robson	65	90	1980–1991
David Beckham	59	115	1996–2009
Steven Gerrard	38	114	2000–2014

He helped United win six Premier League titles and the 1999 Champions League. He also won titles at Real Madrid. After four years there, Beckham made a surprise transfer to American team LA Galaxy, where he helped improve the quality of play, and the attendances, in the league. Beckham then transferred to AC Milan and Paris Saint-Germain. He is the first English player to win league titles in four countries: England, Spain, France and the USA.

His work ethic – as well as his natural good looks – meant companies asked him to endorse their products. He signed a lifetime contract with Adidas and has modelled for brands like Pepsi, Disney and H&M underwear – he was even pictured on the side of a bus in his pants! Other players, such as Ronaldo, learned that football stars can have a global reach and they are now sponsored by brands across the world. Beckham was one of the first to do this.

Even though he stopped playing in 2013, he remains just as famous since his retirement. Now he travels the world as a UNICEF Goodwill Ambassador and is dedicated to helping disadvantaged children. He paved the way for today's footballers to be so famous; more importantly, he now uses his own celebrity to help others.

STAR PLAYER

LUCY BRONZE

Determined England defender now one of the world's best

Born: 1991
Country: England
Position: Defender
Major clubs: Everton, Liverpool, Manchester City (all England), Lyon (France)
International highlights: Semi-finalist, 2015 World Cup; semi-finalist, 2017 Euros

STAR STAT

1st
English player to win Women's Champions League

Key | = leader | = innovator | = scorer | = stopper

Lucy Bronze made up for lost time after missing two years with knee injuries that almost ended her football career before it began. She was told she might lose a leg, but she ended up as one of the top stars of the England team and is the first English player to win the Women's Champions League. She was nominated for the women's Ballon D'Or in 2018. This Bronze deserves gold!

Bronze loved maths as a girl and wanted to become an accountant. But football added up for her and she started out at local club Sunderland, helping them reach the 2009 Women's FA Cup final. She went on to win league titles with Liverpool and Manchester City. As a right-back she tackled aggressively, pushed forward to join attacks and scored a huge number of goals given her position. England coach Phil Neville described her as four players rolled into one!

She helped England reach two semi-finals: in the 2015 Women's World Cup – thanks to her winning goals in knock-out matches against Norway and Canada – and the 2017 Euros.

Bronze always challenges herself. She has won lots of individual awards, which is rare for a defender, but she wanted to compete at the highest possible level with her club. So in 2017, she signed for top French club Lyon, where she learned a new language, improved as a player and won the Champions League trophy in her first season. *Magnifique!*

"I JUST WANT TO CHALLENGE MYSELF ALL THE TIME ... BY GOING TO DIFFERENT CLUBS, ENVIRONMENTS AND PLAYING WITH DIFFERENT PLAYERS."

Lucy Bronze

STAR PLAYER

ROGÉRIO CENI

Highest-scoring goalkeeper of all time

STAR STAT

129 goals scored

Born: 1973
Country: Brazil
Position: Goalkeeper
Major clubs: São Paulo (Brazil)
International highlights: Winner, 2002 World Cup; played in 2006 World Cup

Key | = leader | = innovator | = scorer | = stopper

The Brazilian keeper Rogério Ceni was great at saving goals. He was also brilliant at scoring them! His career total stands at 129 goals in competitive games, the record number for a goalkeeper. They consisted of 69 penalties, 59 free kicks and one when he was passed the ball from a free kick.

When Ceni started out as a professional, he had no idea that he would have a talent for shooting. In his early twenties, his coach at Brazilian club São Paulo spotted that he had a good way of kicking the ball and suggested he practise penalties and free kicks. He took 15,000 practice shots in six months (that's almost 100 a day), before the coach gave him a chance in a real game. Aged 24 he scored a free kick for the first time and became the club's free-kick and penalty specialist.

Ceni was also good at defending his own goal. He was in the Brazil squad at two World Cups. At São Paulo, he twice won the Copa Libertadores (the South American version of the Champions League), and in 2005 was Man of the Match when the club beat Liverpool in the final of the FIFA Club World Cup.

Ceni, a calm and courageous presence on the pitch, was a giant for his team. He played 1,237 times for São Paulo over 23 seasons, the most appearances a professional footballer has ever made for the same club. He has the record for captaining the same team for the most games (982) and for winning the most games at the same club (601). When it comes to football records, this owner of the number 1 shirt is number one!

STAR PLAYER

Sir BOBBY CHARLTON

Midfield hero who brought it home for England in 1966

Born: 1937
Country: England
Position: Midfielder
Major clubs: Manchester United (England)
International highlights: Scored in 1962 World Cup; winner, 1966 World Cup
Individual awards: Winner, 1966 Ballon D'Or

STAR STAT

3

goals scored in the 1966 World Cup

Key | = leader | = innovator | = scorer | = stopper

With his surging runs and trademark blistering shots from outside the area, Bobby Charlton was the outstanding English player of his generation. He won all that there was to win: including the World Cup, the European Cup (the forerunner to the Champions League), and the Ballon D'Or, the world's most prestigious award for individual performance.

Charlton spent almost his entire career at Manchester United, which he joined aged fifteen as a youth player. He was one of the Busby Babes, a crop of young players developed at the club under the supervision of coach Matt Busby. Aged 20, he was an established member of the first team. As England champions, United were England's sole representatives in the European Cup. Then tragedy struck.

In February 1958, Manchester United's plane crashed when attempting to take off from Munich airport. The team were on their way home from playing Red Star Belgrade in the European Cup quarter-final. The plane was slowed by slush on the runway. It skidded through a fence, crossed a road, crashed into a house and split in two. Charlton was unconscious when he was dragged from the wreckage. Of the 44 people who were in the plane, 23 died, including eight United players, three United staff and eight journalists who had been covering the game.

"IN THE SWEEP OF ITS APPEAL, ITS ABILITY TO TOUCH EVERY CORNER OF HUMANITY, FOOTBALL IS THE ONLY GAME THAT NEEDED TO BE INVENTED."

Bobby Charlton

The tragedy shocked the world. Charlton, who suffered just a gash on his head, was so traumatised by the event that he was only able to properly speak about it years afterwards. Yet barely a month after the crash, he was back playing football. He was only 20 years old, but as one of the best surviving players of what was England's top team at the time, the spotlight was on him like never before. He was the player around whom the new Manchester United team would be built.

The young Charlton coped with the pressure and became a world-class footballer. He was exciting to watch: an elegant, versatile player who could dribble, shoot with either foot and score stunning goals. Off the pitch, he was a reliable, modest and serious man.

Charlton was at the heart of the England team that achieved their greatest ever trophy: the 1966 World Cup. He scored England's first goal in the tournament, in a 2–0

win against Mexico but, more importantly, he netted both in the 2–1 against Portugal in the semi-final. He was awarded the Golden Ball, for the tournament's best player. The same year he won the Ballon D'Or.

With Charlton as captain, surrounded by a new generation of Busby Babes, Manchester United regained its dominance. In 1968, exactly ten seasons after the Munich crash, United became the first English team to win the European Cup. Charlton scored two goals in the final and, since he was captain, he became the first Englishman to lift the trophy.

He remains the embodiment of England footballing excellence: a great player and also an inspiring leader, who led his club from its worst moment to its greatest triumph.

STAR PLAYER

BRANDI CHASTAIN

Penalty hero who is donating her brain to science

Born: 1968
Country: USA
Position: Midfielder, then defender
Major clubs: San Jose CyberRays (USA)
International highlights: Winner, 1991 World Cup; winner, 1999 World Cup

STAR STAT

90,185

fans in stadium watching 1999 World Cup final

Key | = leader | = innovator | = scorer | = stopper

Brandi Chastain scored the penalty that won the 1999 Women's World Cup for the USA. Her spontaneous and powerful celebration, which was shown all around the world, helped football become popular as a women's sport in the USA.

Chastain started playing football aged eight and first played for the boys' team, as there wasn't a girls' team at her school. She just wanted to play and she didn't care who with! When she moved to high school, she played for a girls' team, and won three championship titles in a row.

At home, she used to kick a ball against a wall for hours with both feet, until she was just as good with her left foot as her right foot. Her grandfather rewarded her when she played in junior games, paying her $1 for every goal and $1.50 for every assist. Her practice paid off when she was the only true two-footed player in the USA side that hosted the 1999 World Cup. She was playing in defence, after converting from midfield. USA reached the final against China and it went to a penalty shoot-out. USA coach Tony DiCicco told Chastain to take the fifth, and potentially decisive, penalty. He had one piece of advice.

DiCicco knew that Chastain had more power with her right foot, but more accuracy with her left foot. With the stakes this high, accuracy was more important.

The stadium was silent as Chastain walked to the penalty spot. There were over 90,000 home fans watching, and all she could hear was her own breathing. "It was slow-motion between my foot and the net," she told us. "It seemed to take for ever and while the ball travelled, everything was so quiet and still and slow. And when it hit the net: an explosion! Noise, cheering, cameras, team-mates, everything."

Chastain fell to her knees and ripped off her shirt, waving it around her head. Photos of her wearing her black sports bra, crying with joy, with biceps bulging as she pumped her fists, were shown on magazine covers. She looked strong, powerful and triumphant, and her celebration became a defining moment for women's football. Suddenly young girls across the USA were inspired and wanted to get involved. Chastain helped by setting up sports charities to introduce disadvantaged children to the game she loved.

Chastain has devoted her life to football. She will also do the same after her death, by donating her brain to researchers at Boston University's Concussion Legacy Foundation.

Scientists want to find out if heading the ball numerous times (and Chastain really did win a lot of headers) from a young age causes problems in your brain when you get older.

Chastain has played football for 40 years and thinks her brain may contain some clues. She said, "I won't need it then... It would be something that could protect and save some kids."

Her heroic actions could be as important after her life as during it. What a brainiac!

STAR PLAYER

DAVID CLARKE

Blind centre-forward with inspiring attitude to life and goals

STAR STATS

Born: 1970
Country: England
Position: Centre-forward
International highlights: Played in 6 World Cups and 7 Euros
Individual awards: Winner of 5 Golden Boot awards

128
goals scored for England

Key | = leader | = innovator | = scorer | = stopper

David Clarke lost his eyesight when he was a boy but he never let that stand in the way of his dreams. He played as a centre-forward for England's blind team, scoring 128 goals in 144 international matches. He played in six World Cups and seven Euros, winning the Golden Boot for tournament top scorer on five occasions.

Clarke showed incredible dedication to play for England. His mantra was: "Why would you not want to be the best person you can be?" He trained in the morning at 6 a.m. and in the evening at 6 p.m., and in between had a job in a bank. He needed to be good at maths to keep track of all his goals!

Clarke's last-minute back-heeled assist set up the goal that qualified England for the 2008 Paralympics in Beijing. It was a crucial moment in the sport's development, and convinced the FA to continue funding blind football. Clarke was the team's talisman, their leader on the pitch, and he proudly carried the torch at London's Olympic Stadium to open the 2012 Paralympics. The England team, watched by millions, competed against the world's best.

Clarke retired after that tournament but his legacy was secure. The FA now has a purpose-built blind football pitch at the national training centre and a changing room named after Clarke. Thanks to him, the sport is now a professional career choice for a blind person.

THE RULES OF BLIND FOOTBALL

Five-a-side with rolling subs.

Balls have ball bearings in them, which rattle, so players know where the ball is.

Each team has a guide behind the goal who can shout instructions to players.

Goalkeepers are fully or partially sighted.

The team coach is allowed to coach in the middle third of the pitch.

STAR PLAYER

LIV COOKE

Freestyle champion who is inspiring a new generation

Born: 1999
Country: England
Position: Any, even upside down!
International highlights: Finalist, 2016 World Freestyle Football Championships; winner, 2017 World Freestyle Football Championships

STAR STAT

2,000

times she practises each trick

Key | = leader | = innovator | = scorer | = stopper

> "HOW GOOD YOU ARE DEPENDS ON HOW MUCH WORK YOU PUT IN."
>
> Liv Cooke

Liv Cooke turned a setback into an advantage. After a back injury ended her dreams of becoming a professional footballer, she put all her energies into a different sport – and became its youngest ever world champion.

Cooke was a youth player at Blackburn Rovers when, at fifteen, she suffered recurring back pain. Unable to stand up for long periods, she was able to practise her ball skills sitting down and fell in love with a new way of playing football. Training for five hours a day, six days a week, she mastered amazing skills and, at seventeen, became Britain's first professional female freestyler.

Freestyle football is a cross between keepy-uppies and gymnastics, with players performing incredible tricks by bouncing the ball on any part of their body. Freestylers need balance, creativity, composure, technique, flexibility, confidence – and of course brilliant ball skills. Cooke says she practises a set of tricks 2,000 times before a competition. In 2017, she became freestyle world champion, with moves that were tougher and better executed than all her opponents.

Cooke says she is only the world's best because she works the hardest, an attitude that is inspiring to a generation of girls who love football. She has freestyled on a fishing boat in Norway, in a war-torn house in Dubrovnik, and surrounded by sheep on a remote Scottish island. But her dream remains to freestyle in Rome's Colosseum. This gladiator wants to conquer the world!

STAR PLAYER

JOHAN CRUYFF

Football-thinker who dazzled as both a player and coach

Born: 1947
Died: 2016
Country: Netherlands
Position: Attacking midfielder
Major clubs: Ajax (Netherlands), Barcelona (Spain)
International highlights (as player): Finalist, 1974 World Cup
Individual awards: Winner, 1971, 1973, 1974 Ballon D'Or

STAR STAT

14
shirt number at Ajax

Key | = leader | = innovator | = scorer | = stopper

Johan Cruyff was arguably the most influential player in the history of football. Not only was he the best European player of his generation, but he introduced and developed a style of attacking football that was so successful it is still used by many top teams today.

Cruyff grew up in Amsterdam near Ajax's stadium. He joined the club's youth team aged ten and made his first-team debut aged seventeen. He had brilliant technical skills, speed and acceleration, but what was really special about him was his vision and tactical understanding. Under the guidance of coach Rinus Michels, he invented a new way of playing, called Total Football, in which the outfield players in the team were able to swap positions. This new attacking style meant that the team were always creating new opportunities to move forward and confuse the opposition.

With Cruyff leading the way on the pitch, Ajax went from Dutch also-rans to European champions. In seven full seasons at the club, he won the Dutch league six times and the European Cup (the forerunner to the Champions League) three times. This Dutchman was flying!

Total Football was also transforming the fortunes of the Netherlands national team, who had not been to a World Cup for almost four decades until Cruyff led his country to the final of the 1974 World Cup. Even though, unluckily, they lost to West Germany, Cruyff was named player of the tournament and his Dutch side are remembered as one of the most exciting World Cup teams ever. That year, Cruyff won his third Ballon D'Or, making him the first player to win three.

"WINNING IS AN IMPORTANT THING, BUT TO HAVE YOUR OWN STYLE, TO HAVE PEOPLE COPY YOU, TO ADMIRE YOU, THAT IS THE GREATEST GIFT."
Johan Cruyff

In 1973, Cruyff transferred to Barcelona for what was then a world-record fee. In his first season, Barça won La Liga for the first time in fourteen years, and it was the beginning of a deep connection with the club that would last all his life.

After retiring as a player, Cruyff became a coach. He fitted the role perfectly. Not only did he have innovative ideas about the game but he was also brilliant at spotting and motivating young players. He started his coaching career at Ajax and three years later, in 1988, he moved back to Barcelona, which at that point was a club in crisis.

Cruyff remade the club in his image, building up a side that played according to his philosophy of possession-based attacking football. He won many trophies, including four La Ligas in a row. But it was about more than the silverware. Cruyff's importance to Barcelona was in developing a winning mentality for the club, and establishing a playing style which is still very influential to how many top teams play. It was also Cruyff's idea to establish a youth academy to teach youngsters to play the Barça way. La Masia has since produced many amazing players, including Lionel Messi.

Cruyff used to say that football is a game you play with your brain. He certainly used his – both on the pitch and off it!

CRUYFF'S COMMANDMENTS

1. To accomplish things, you have to do them together.
2. Take care of things as if they were your own.
3. Respect one another.
4. Involve others in your activities.
5. Dare to try something new.
6. Always help each other within a team.
7. Be yourself.
8. Interaction is crucial, both in sport and in life.
9. Know the basics.
10. Know what to do.
11. Sport strengthens body and soul.
12. Try to learn something new every day.
13. Playing together is an essential part of any game.
14. Bring beauty to the sport.

STAR PLAYER

Sir KENNY DALGLISH

Scotland and Liverpool hero who became a king of compassion

STAR STAT

30 goals scored for Scotland

Born: 1951
Country: Scotland
Position: Forward
Major clubs: Celtic (Scotland), Liverpool (England)
International highlights: Played in 1974 World Cup; scored in 1978 World Cup; scored in 1982 World Cup

Key | = leader | = innovator | = scorer | = stopper

Kenny Dalglish was loved for what he did on the pitch, and became even more loved for what he did off it. A key member of the Liverpool team that dominated English and European football in the late 1970s and 1980s, he is considered by Reds fans to be the club's greatest ever player.

> "THEY SUPPORTED LIVERPOOL. NOW IT IS THE TURN OF LIVERPOOL FOOTBALL CLUB TO SUPPORT THEM."
>
> Kenny Dalglish on Liverpool fans after Hillsborough

Yet the moment that most marked his life was not a sporting triumph but a tragedy: the Hillsborough disaster of 1989, in which 96 Liverpool fans died. In the aftermath, Dalglish supported the families of the victims and helped them campaign for justice.

Born and bred in Glasgow, Dalglish was already a legend at Celtic when, in 1977, he was signed by Liverpool for what was then the largest amount of money ever paid for a British player. He showed his worth almost immediately, scoring seven minutes into his league debut. In his first season at Liverpool, the club won the European Cup (the forerunner of the Champions League), with Dalglish scoring the only goal in the final.

The trophy haul in this period at Anfield was unbelievable. Fans called him King Kenny for good reason. Liverpool won the league in six of Dalglish's first nine years at the club, and the European Cup three times. He was a prolific scorer with incredible vision and took as much pleasure in creating goals for his team-mates as scoring himself.

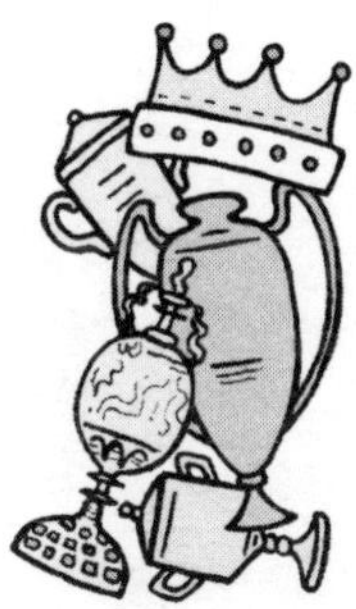

In 1985, he took on the role of coach as well as player. That season, Liverpool won the league and cup double for the first time, with Dalglish scoring the title-winning goal on the last day of the season.

Dalglish was coach when, in 1989, the Liverpool team went to the Hillsborough stadium in Sheffield for an FA Cup semi-final against Nottingham Forest. Shortly before kick-off, thousands of Liverpool fans were allowed to enter the standing area of the stadium. The area was too small to cope with such a large number of people and was surrounded by a high fence to stop fans accessing the pitch. In the crush, 96 fans were killed and hundreds injured. The horrific scenes played out in full view of the crowds and a live TV audience.

Since most of the fatalities were from Liverpool, the city was consumed with grief. Dalglish went out of his way to help the bereaved, making sure that he or a club representative was at every funeral. Sometimes he went to several funerals a day.

He was also a strong and public voice for Liverpool, dismissing false allegations that the fans were somehow responsible for the tragedy. He embodied the words of Liverpool's anthem "You'll Never Walk Alone" as he was there when the fans needed him most.

The trauma and stress of dealing with so much sadness took their toll on Dalglish's mental and physical health, and ultimately led to him resigning from Liverpool. He returned to coaching later, leading Blackburn Rovers to the Premier League title in 1995.

In 2017, Liverpool renamed one of their stands the Kenny Dalglish Stand as a tribute not only to his football achievements, but also because of how he supported the community after Hillsborough. For the same reasons, he was given a knighthood in 2018. Arise, Sir Kenny!

STAR PLAYER

DIDIER DESCHAMPS

Born leader who inspired Les Bleus to double World Cup glory

Born: 1968
Country: France
Position: Midfielder
Major clubs (as player): Marseille (France), Juventus (Italy), Chelsea (England)
International highlights: (as player): Winner, 1998 World Cup; winner, 2000 Euros
International highlights: (as coach): Finalist, 2016 Euros; winner, 2018 World Cup

STAR STAT

52

matches played as France captain

Key | = leader | = innovator | = scorer | = stopper

Didier Deschamps is the architect of the two greatest successes in France's football history – as captain of the team that won its first World Cup, in 1998, and coach of the team that won its second, in 2018. He was not a spectacular player, but what made him excel were his unparalleled leadership skills, which played a vital role in both triumphs.

> "I DON'T THINK YOU JUST BECOME A LEADER. IT'S SOMETHING YOU'RE BORN WITH, AND COMES FROM HOW YOU ARE AS THE ONE WHO INFLUENCES THINGS."
>
> Didier Deschamps

Deschamps spent his whole career playing as a defensive midfielder – a position that allowed him to see almost the whole pitch in front of him. A born leader, he captained every team for which he was a regular starter, beginning at his first club, Aviron Bayonnais, where he wore the armband aged eleven in a team of thirteen-to-fifteen-year-olds.

He moved to the Nantes academy when he was fourteen, and in the holidays would visit his parents' neighbour, an osteopath, who taught him how to stretch his muscles in preparation for matches and to prevent injury. Learning how to take care of his body paid off, as Deschamps was never seriously injured in his career, a rare achievement for players at this level.

He was made Nantes captain at nineteen, and was put in charge of players almost twice his age. "If I had something to say, it was always for the good of the team," Deschamps told us. "My team-mates accepted my leadership."

So what made Deschamps such a good leader? The man himself says these are the most important skills:

For Deschamps, winning was more important than skilful tricks and flicks. Eric Cantona, a flamboyant former team-mate at Marseille and France, once described Deschamps as a "water-carrier". The suggestion was that Deschamps lacked the skill to excite fans, and just did the legwork for his more creative team-mates. The fact is that without Deschamps the French team most likely would not have won anything. As one coach put it: "Zidane does not need anyone else to win the Ballon D'Or, but he needs Deschamps to win trophies."

And Deschamps won plenty. He was Marseille captain when they became the first (and, to date, only) French team to win the Champions League; at Juventus, he won three league titles and one Champions League. He returned to both clubs as a coach, winning the French league with Marseille and the second division for Juventus (who had just been relegated after a match-fixing scandal).

Deschamps took over as France coach in 2012, when support for the national team was at an all-time low. France had under-performed in a series of tournaments and the fans were fed up. Deschamps restored the relationship by making fans proud of the team again. France came close to winning the 2016 European Championship on home soil, but lost 1–0 to Portugal in the final. Deschamps used that disappointment to inspire his team two years later. In the 2018 World Cup, France swept past Argentina (4–3), Uruguay (2–0), Belgium (1–0) and, in the final, Croatia (4–2) to be crowned the best team in the world. It helped that they had the best leader to inspire them. Bravo, Didier!

STAR PLAYER

DIDIER DROGBA

African great who helped end civil war in his homeland

Born: 1978
Country: Ivory Coast
Position: Centre-forward
Major clubs: Marseille (France), Chelsea (England), Galatasaray (Turkey), Montreal Impact (Canada)
International highlights: Finalist, 2006 Africa Cup of Nations; scored in 2010 World Cup; finalist, 2012 Africa Cup of Nations; played in 2014 World Cup

STAR STAT

65
goals scored for Ivory Coast

Key | = leader | = innovator | = scorer | = stopper

Didier Drogba is proof of the positive effects football can bring to the world. The talented centre-forward had Champions League success at Chelsea, but an even sweeter victory was helping to bring about peace in his home country.

When Drogba was playing for the Ivory Coast national team, the country was divided by a brutal civil war that had killed thousands of people. After the team qualified for the 2006 World Cup, Drogba made an emotional plea to the different groups fighting across the country to lay down their weapons. He then helped behind the scenes to bring about peace. It worked: Drogba said that politicians had divided the country but the football team had managed to unite them. In doing so, he probably saved many lives.

"I HAVE WON MANY TROPHIES IN MY TIME, BUT NOTHING WILL EVER TOP HELPING WIN THE BATTLE FOR PEACE IN MY COUNTRY."
Didier Drogba

Drogba was just as effective on the pitch. He was a natural leader, greatly loved at all of his clubs, starting at Levallois, then Le Mans, Guingamp, Marseille, Chelsea, Shanghai Shenhua, Galatasaray, Montreal Impact and Phoenix Rising. Levallois even named their ground the Stade Didier Drogba in his honour.

It was at Chelsea that Drogba turned into one of the most feared centre-forwards in the world. His smart movement, brilliant finishing and strength in the air was every defender's worst nightmare. He won four Premier League titles with Chelsea and scored goals in seven Cup finals. He was in seventh heaven!

DROGBA'S VICTORIES

YEAR	CUP	FINAL OPPONENT	FINAL SCORE
2005	League Cup	Liverpool	3–2
2007	League Cup	Arsenal	2–1
2007	FA Cup	Manchester United	1–0
2009	FA Cup	Everton	2–1
2010	FA Cup	Portsmouth	1–0
2012	FA Cup	Liverpool	2–1
2012	Champions League	Bayern Munich	1–1

Drogba's biggest dream at Chelsea was to help the club win the Champions League for the first time. He came close in 2008, making the final against Manchester United. But Drogba was sent off in a dramatic finale, so was not able to take part in the penalty shoot-out that Chelsea lost. The following year, he was so distressed after a semi-final defeat to Barcelona that he was fined for criticising the referee.

His last opportunity came in the 2012 final against Bayern Munich, on their home turf in Germany. Bayern were 1–0 ahead with less than a minute to play when Drogba rose highest to glance home a corner to level the scores. The game went to penalties and, you guessed it, Drogba stroked home the winning spot kick! It was even more special because Drogba had waited so long for the moment to come. He finally won the trophy he had wanted for years.

That victory was even sweeter because, earlier that year, Drogba had lost another penalty shoot-out: this time with Ivory Coast in the final of the Africa Cup of Nations. He never did win a major trophy with his country – but no other player can claim to have brought peace to their country, which is much more important!

STAR PLAYER

EDIN DŽEKO

Boy who survived a war to become a European top centre-forward

Born: 1986
Country: Bosnia and Herzegovina
Position: Centre-forward
Major clubs: Wolfsburg (Germany), Manchester City (England), Roma (Italy)
International highlights: Scored in 2014 World Cup

STAR STAT

5
European leagues he has played in

Key | = leader | = innovator | = scorer | = stopper

Bosnian forward Edin Džeko's journey to the top is one of bravery and strength. He is the first person to score 50 goals or more in three of Europe's top five leagues: that's 50 for Manchester City in the Premier League, 50 for Wolfsburg in the Bundesliga and 50 for Roma in Serie A. Several centre-forwards have made names for themselves in two top leagues, but the triple 50 is unique!

Yet Džeko's European success story could very easily have been a tale of tragedy. Between the ages of six and ten, he lived in a war zone. Between 1992 and 1996, his home city in Bosnia, Sarajevo, was under siege. Soldiers surrounded the city, stopping anyone from leaving it and food and medical supplies from getting in. Buildings were bombed relentlessly, including Džeko's home. The people of Sarajevo didn't know if they would live or die.

"WAR MAKES YOU GROW UP FASTER."
Edin Džeko

Džeko's mother remembers a time when he asked to play football outside. She had sensed something was wrong and said no. Minutes later a bomb exploded in the field where he would have been playing. Džeko was lucky to survive, but the siege claimed thousands of lives. "We lost friends and relatives," Džeko said. "The memory doesn't leave you." He learned to play football indoors, with sandbags around the window.

Only once the siege came to an end was he able to play in the streets. Such was the scale of devastation, that one of the city's clubs, Zeljeznicar, had to clear unexploded mines from their pitch.

Džeko made his debut for Zeljeznicar aged eighteen. Fans thought he was a too-tall target man with not much of a future. But Džeko believed his experiences during the war had made him stronger. His coach, Jiri Plisek, agreed, saying: "Džeko had that mental attitude to the game that makes a player special." When Plisek, who is Czech, moved to a club in the Czech Republic, he insisted that Džeko came with him. Soon Džeko was performing so well that he was offered Czech nationality so he could play for the national team. This was an enticing offer: the Czech Republic has an established national team, whereas Bosnia is a minnow. Yet Džeko turned the offer down, remaining loyal to his home country.

In 2007, Džeko transferred to Wolfsburg in Germany, where he scored 66 goals in 111 appearances, helping them win the Bundesliga for the first time in the club's history. He and his team-mate, Grafite, became the highest scoring duo in the Bundesliga. Džeko turned down another offer, this time to play for the German team. He wanted to stay with Bosnia, even though at that time his home country had never managed to qualify for the Euros or a World Cup. For Džeko, his Bosnian identity was more important than even the greatest football glory, and this patriotism helped turn him into a national symbol, nicknamed Bosnian Diamond.

Between 2011 and 2015, Džeko played for Manchester City, where he got a reputation as a super-sub, often coming off the bench to score vital goals. Then he transferred to Roma, where he topped the scoring charts in Serie A in his second season. The season after, his goals (including one stunning volley against Chelsea) helped Roma reach the Champions League semi-final, where he scored in both legs of a dramatic 6–7 defeat to Liverpool.

Džeko's loyalty to the country of his birth was finally rewarded when he helped Bosnia qualify for the 2014 World Cup. He scored the opening goal in Bosnia's 3–1 defeat of Iran, the country's first World Cup victory.

The little boy who grew up dodging bullets during the Balkan War turned into Bosnia's star player and all-time top scorer – a national hero.

STAR PLAYER

MATHIEU FLAMINI

Midfielder who is helping save the planet

Born: 1984
Country: France
Position: Midfielder
Major clubs: Marseille (France), Arsenal (England), AC Milan (Italy)

STAR STAT

1

Italian league title won with AC Milan

Key | = leader | = innovator | = scorer | = stopper

Mathieu Flamini has always loved the outdoors. When hiking or scuba-diving he often saw rubbish, such as plastic bags, harming the environment. It made him sad and angry, and he wanted to do something about it.

But he also loved football. Flamini was a youth player with his hometown club, Marseille. In 2004, he moved to Arsenal and, in 2008, he signed with AC Milan. Later he returned to Arsenal for a further three seasons.

Back in London, Flamini revealed a secret to his team-mates: he had become a businessman! His team-mates had been baffled by why the Frenchman often showed up for training in a suit – now they understood.

Flamini had founded a company, GF Biochemicals, which turns waste material from farms, such as wood, into a chemical called levulinic acid. The levulinic acid is then turned into household products like detergents and plastics.

The business has nothing to do with football, but concerns itself with another of Flamini's passions: how to make our planet a cleaner place. Most detergents and plastics are made from petrol. If these products are made instead from farm waste, we are saving resources by recycling material that would otherwise be thrown away. It also means we use less petrol, which is a good thing because petrol harms the environment.

Flamini may not have been captain at Arsenal or Milan, but he is turning into a captain of industry!

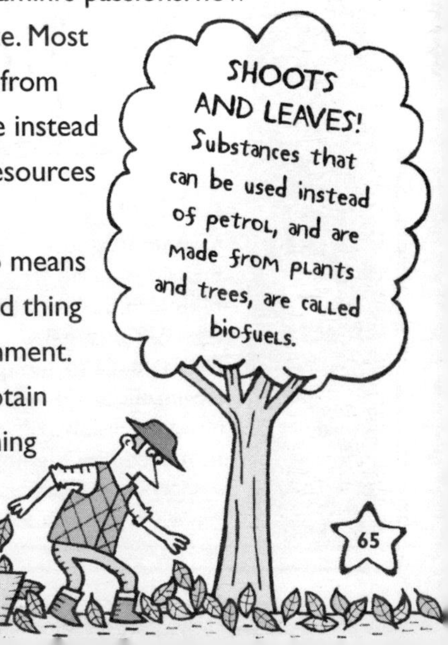

STAR PLAYER

PEP GUARDIOLA

Tactical genius who constantly innovates to improve players

Born: 1971
Country: Spain
Position: Midfielder
Major clubs (as player): Barcelona (Spain), Roma (Italy)
Major clubs (as coach): Barcelona (Spain), Bayern Munich (Germany), Manchester City (England)
International highlights (as coach): Winner, 2009 Champions League; winner, 2011 Champions League

STAR STAT

14
trophies won in four years as Barcelona coach

Key | = leader | = innovator | = scorer | = stopper

Former midfielder Pep Guardiola is an inspiring, revolutionary and extremely successful coach, who has reinvented how we think about football tactics. As a coach, he has won league titles in three different countries, and been credited for the World Cup victories of two of them.

Josep "Pep" Guardiola was born just outside Barcelona. His father, Valenti, taught young Pep the importance of hard work, humility and integrity. Pep's career began at thirteen, when he joined La Masia, the Barcelona youth academy set up by the club's coach Johan Cruyff. Guardiola described his six years there as "the best years of my life".

Cruyff converted young Guardiola into a defensive midfielder, able to watch the whole match play out in front of him. As a Barcelona player, he won six La Liga titles and the 1994 European Cup (the forerunner to the Champions League). Guardiola officially stopped playing in 2006, but even before then he spent time with influential coaches who helped him develop a style for his teams to play. Above all, Guardiola credits Cruyff for his approach to coaching and has admitted to thinking in the middle of matches, "What would Johan do?" The pair used to spend hours discussing football, and agreed on certain things:

> “I AM NOT DEALING WITH FOOTBALLERS, I AM DEALING WITH PEOPLE ... I HAVE TO MAKE THEM SEE THAT WITHOUT EACH OTHER THEY ARE NOTHING.”
>
> Pep Guardiola

Guardiola was 37 and had been a reserve coach for only a year when Barcelona appointed him head coach in 2008. It was seen as a risk, but it worked spectacularly. In his first season, Guardiola won an unprecedented six trophies, becoming the youngest coach to lift the Champions League. His Barcelona team played outstanding football and won fourteen trophies in Guardiola’s four years in charge. Guardiola summed up his philosophy very simply: “Take the ball, pass the ball. Take the ball, pass the ball.”

Guardiola is expert at improving players, and often changes their positions to make them better. He did this with Lionel Messi, converting him from a winger into a decoy centre-forward, known as a false nine. Guardiola spends hours watching videos to spot an opposition's weakness. At 10.30 p.m. on the night before Barcelona played rivals Real Madrid, he called Messi into his office and told him about the new false nine position. The next

INSIDE PEP'S MIND LAB

Here are some of the innovations Pep Guardiola used to continue the winning habit:

SIX SECONDS

Guardiola told his Barcelona players to try to win the ball within six seconds of losing it, with high-intensity pressing, to stop attacks and catch opponents out of position.

day, Messi scored twice, as Barcelona beat Real Madrid 6–2. The rest is history: Messi averaged over 52 goals per season playing under Guardiola. (In one season, Messi's 50 league goals were more than what fourteen Spanish teams managed to score all season.)

The Guardiola effect rubbed off onto Spain's national team, who took the same approach to possession when they won the 2010 World Cup with six starters from Barcelona. The same thing happened in Germany, when Guardiola coached Bayern Munich. Again, he improved the individuals at the club and five Bayern players started Germany's triumphant 2014 World Cup final.

Manchester City broke the Premier League record for goals scored and points earned in 2017–18, Guardiola's second season in charge. He continues to push the boundaries of tactical innovation, and demands that his players espouse the same values that his father, Valenti, taught: humility, hard work and putting the team first. As he once put it: "Talent will get you as far as the dressing room – how you behave determines if you stay there."

IN THE ZONE

Guardiola divides the training pitch into twenty zones and drills his players to occupy certain areas at certain points in the game. That's how they know to make the right pass each time.

ALL CHANGE

Guardiola will switch a player's position if he thinks it will give his team more chance of keeping the ball: Javier Mascherano, Philipp Lahm and Fabian Delph have all benefited.

STAR PLAYER

BÉLA GUTTMANN

Superstar coach who had a lucky escape in the Second World War

Born: 1899
Died: 1981
Country: Hungary
Major clubs (as coach): Quilmes (Argentina), AC Milan (Italy), Honvéd (Hungary), São Paulo (Brazil), Porto, Benfica (both Portugal), Peñarol (Uruguay), Panathinaikos (Greece)
International highlights (as coach): Winner, 1961 and 1962 European Cup

STAR STAT

12
countries where he coached professional teams

Key | = leader | = innovator | = scorer | = stopper

Béla Guttmann was the first international superstar coach, a larger-than-life character who, in the 1950s and 1960s, worked at some of the biggest clubs in the world and whose innovative tactics changed the game as we know it.

Born and raised in Hungary, where he started his career as a midfielder for local clubs, Guttmann eventually became a successful coach. In a globe-trotting career, he had 25 coaching jobs in twelve countries across three continents. One of those clubs was São Paulo, in Brazil, where in 1957 he introduced a tactical system new to Brazil: 4-2-4, a hyper-aggressive formation in which six players attack when the team has the ball, and six players defend when the team do not.

The Brazil national team copied Guttmann and started playing 4-2-4. The following year Brazil won its first ever World Cup, meaning that Brazil's famously exciting style of football emerged, in part, because of a Hungarian!

Guttmann's greatest success came when he was coach of Benfica in Portugal. He won the European Cup in both 1961 and 1962. At Benfica he also signed a striker thanks to a recommendation at the barber's. The man having his hair cut next to him told him about a young player called Eusébio who he had spotted in Mozambique. (At that time the African country was a Portuguese colony.) Guttmann raced to sign up Eusébio, who became one of Portugal's greatest ever players.

Guttmann was as famous for being outspoken as he was for his coaching skills. When he won the European Cup for a second time, he resigned, furious because his bosses refused to give him a pay rise, which he felt was unfair. It is said that he told them that Benfica would not win another European trophy for the next one hundred years, and it became known as the "curse" of Béla Guttmann. "I am the most expensive coach in the world, but, looking at my achievements, I'm actually cheap," he said. Since then, Benfica have played in eight European finals and lost EVERY SINGLE ONE.

Guttmann's journey to the top wasn't easy. In search of a coaching job, he moved from the USA to Hungary in 1938. Guttmann was Jewish, and in Hungary at this time, laws were being passed that restricted the freedom and rights of Jewish people. But Guttmann was so passionate about football that he decided to take the coaching job despite the dangers.

Soon after, the German Nazi regime, led by Adolf Hitler, marched into Hungary. The Nazis had declared that Jews were its enemies and forced them into concentration camps, sending many to their deaths. Guttmann hid from the Nazis in an attic above a hairdresser's that belonged to his girlfriend's brother. The Nazis broke in to look for him, but fortunately they didn't find him. However, Guttmann was later forced to do slave labour. Against all odds, he managed to escape.

Guttmann survived the war to become one of the most famous coaches of his time. His achievements changed the way coaches approached their roles and paved the way for high-profile figures with strong personalities, such as Pep Guardiola and José Mourinho.

> During the Second World War, six million Jewish people were killed by the Nazis, including Guttmann's father and sister. This was about two thirds of all the Jews in Europe. The murder of many people because of their race or beliefs is called genocide. The Nazi regime's genocide of Jewish people is known as the Holocaust.

STAR PLAYER

JEFF HALL

Defender whose untimely death helped eradicate a horrific disease

Born: 1929
Died: 1959
Country: England
Position: Right-back
Major clubs: Birmingham City (England)

STAR STAT

17
appearances for England

One day, in March 1959, Jeff Hall felt unwell. The Birmingham City and England right-back was having difficulty swallowing. A doctor diagnosed him with a cold. The following day he played for Birmingham in the league, but he still felt terrible. Two weeks later, he was dead.

Hall had died of polio, an infectious disease that can paralyse the limbs, and in rare cases kill. His death shocked the nation. He was one of England's most famous footballers, having played 227 times for his club and seventeen times for the national team. No one expected an athlete in the peak of health to fall ill and die in a matter of weeks. Yet despite being such a tragic event, his death ended up saving hundreds, if not thousands, of lives.

Polio is preventable. The polio vaccination can protect you from it for life. But, in 1958, hardly any young people had been given the vaccine. Jeff Hall's death showed the public that polio could strike anywhere. Within days, huge queues appeared outside vaccination clinics around the country. By 1961, about two thirds of people in their twenties had been vaccinated.

Jeff Hall's death is now seen as a turning point in the UK's fight against polio. Thanks to the publicity that his death caused, the disease is now eradicated in the UK.

STAR PLAYER

MIA HAMM

Record-breaking goal-scorer who inspired a generation of girls

Born: 1972
Country: USA
Position: Forward
Major clubs: Washington Freedom (USA)
International highlights: Winner, 1991 World Cup; semi-finalist, 1995 World Cup; winner, 1999 World Cup; semi-finalist, 2003 World Cup
Individual awards: Winner, 2001 and 2002 FIFA World Player of the Year

STAR STAT

158

international goals for USA, a world record

Key | = leader | = innovator | = scorer | = stopper

Mia Hamm was USA's best player when they won two World Cups and two Olympic golds and is considered the trailblazer who made football popular in the USA. She played in the first Women's World Cup in 1991, in the first women's football event at the 1996 Olympics, and in USA's first World Cup victory in 1999.

When Hamm was very young, her parents moved from Alabama in the south of America to Italy, because her father was a pilot in the US Air Force. Her siblings were sporty, but Hamm had to overcome tough odds even to be able to run and kick a ball. She was born with a partial club foot, which is when the foot rotates inwards and can limit mobility. She had to wear special shoes to correct it.

She kicked her first ball in Italy and fell in love with football. When the family returned to America, she played for her school team – a boys' team, because the girls did not have one.

"TRUE CHAMPIONS AREN'T ALWAYS THE ONES THAT WIN, BUT ARE THOSE WITH THE MOST GUTS."
Mia Hamm

Hamm was only fifteen when she made her debut for the newly formed USA women's national team, known as the USWNT, in 1987. She quickly became the star of the team, but this didn't stop her from getting nervous, sometimes even sick, before matches. She found taking a penalty in the 1999 Women's World Cup final shoot-out so stressful that she missed the celebration party as she fainted in the dressing room after the game. She ended her career with a world-record 158 goals in 275 games for USA.

Hamm never liked doing the interviews and photo shoots that were expected of the team star. She would always talk about the importance of her team-mates and, before one tournament, only agreed to appear on the cover of a magazine if five team-mates joined her.

Her career coincided with the evolution of women's football, and she was at the forefront of its development. She became an icon for girls who wanted to play sport and would travel the country putting on training sessions and giving motivational talks to inspire a new generation of female players.

After she stopped playing, Hamm wanted to stay involved in football. In 2015, she was appointed as a director of Italian side AS Roma, whose American owner praised her knowledge of player development, coaching and charity work. Unsurprisingly, Roma soon launched its official women's team. Hamm combines this job with being the joint-owner of American club Los Angeles FC. These important positions, where she can use her influence to make football a force for good, have led to her being called one of the most powerful women in football.

Her life hasn't been without tragedy. Her older brother Garrett was a talented sportsman who helped Hamm discover her love of football. But he was diagnosed with a rare bone marrow disease when he was sixteen. Hamm was heartbroken when Garrett died aged 28 in 1997. She went on to set up the Mia Hamm Foundation with two aims: to help people who need transplants and to increase opportunities for young women in sport.

Hamm was a winner on the pitch, but her impact off it has been even greater.

UNITED STATES OF A-MIA-CA

Mia Hamm helped the USA become the most successful women's team in world football, with three World Cup wins. Here's how they did it:

1985	First match, a 1–0 defeat to Italy
1991	First FIFA Women's World Cup, beating Norway 2–1 in the final
1999	Second World Cup success, on home soil, sends football popularity soaring
2012	Record fourth Olympic football gold, beating Japan in the final
2015	Carli Lloyd hat-trick in 5–2 victory over Japan secures third World Cup

STAR PLAYER

ADA HEGERBERG

Record-breaking scorer who puts her principles first

Born: 1995
Country: Norway
Position: Forward
Major clubs: Lyon (France)
International highlights: Finalist, 2013 Euros; scored in 2015 World Cup
Individual awards: Winner, 2018 Ballon D'Or

STAR STAT

15
age she debuted in Norwegian First Division

Key | = leader | = innovator | = scorer | = stopper

Norwegian forward Ada Hegerberg is the closest thing to a guarantee of goals. Her strikes have helped Lyon win the French league and the Women's Champions League for three years running. In 2018, she was the first recipient of the Ballon D'Or for the world's best female player. She even slept with the golden trophy on the night she won it!

Hegerberg has won everything she can win in club football. But she is unlikely to repeat that trophy haul on the international scene: she stopped playing for the Norway national team in 2017 because she was dismayed at how women's football was run in her country. Her principles came before any title – even the World Cup.

The men's game in Norway receives more than ten times the funding of the women's game. "Football is the biggest sport in Norway for girls and has been for years, but at the same time girls don't have the same opportunities as the boys," she said. "It's all about how we respect women's football. I wouldn't be the player I am today if I didn't stand up for my values and what I believe in. You have to take some tough decisions to stay true to yourself. I know I have a voice, and I want to use that voice as much as I can to bring things forward." Standing up for what she believed in meant Hegerberg declined to play in the 2019 Women's World Cup.

Hegerberg comes from a family of footballers. Her parents both played and coached, while her elder siblings, Silas and Andrine, played professionally. She was dragged along to play with them and it quickly became apparent that Hegerberg was extremely talented. She was only fifteen when she first played in the top division for Norwegian side Kolbotn, and one year later became the youngest player to score a hat-trick. Big sis Andrine was one of her team-mates! The sisters stuck together and moved to Stabaek, where Hegerberg scored a hat-trick in their victorious 2012 Norwegian Cup final.

They also played together for Norway. Hegerberg made her senior Norway debut at sixteen and was still a teenager when she scored three goals and was voted Best Young Player at the 2015 Women's World Cup.

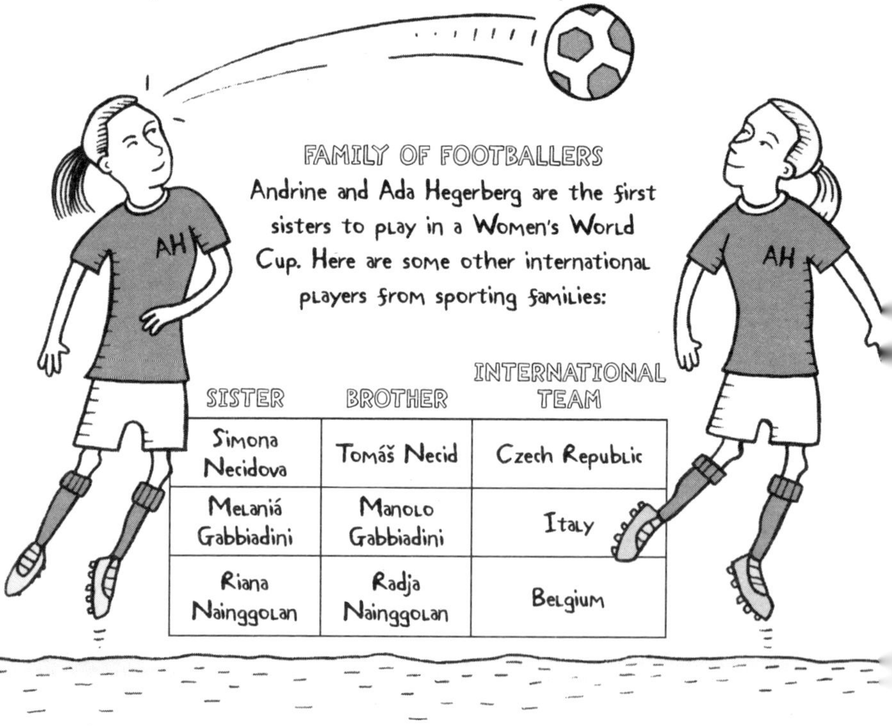

FAMILY OF FOOTBALLERS

Andrine and Ada Hegerberg are the first sisters to play in a Women's World Cup. Here are some other international players from sporting families:

SISTER	BROTHER	INTERNATIONAL TEAM
Simona Necidova	Tomáš Necid	Czech Republic
Melaniá Gabbiadini	Manolo Gabbiadini	Italy
Riana Nainggolan	Radja Nainggolan	Belgium

It was after Hegerberg signed for Lyon that her scoring went stratospheric. She top-scored in the French First Division for three straight seasons, and netted a record fifteen goals in one season in the Women's Champions League as the French champions dominated the European game.

Playing for such a strong team has improved Hegerberg's game. Her eye for goal has always been instinctive and she scores with her right foot, left foot and her head. She is also tactically versatile, able to hold the ball up to bring team-mates into play, and she has the speed and smart movement to play alongside a strike partner.

Hegerberg knows that if she is happy and confident, she will be a better player and person. As a way of taking her mind off football, she is an avid reader. She loves books! We suggest she adds *Football School* to her reading list – then this scoring sensation will be even happier!

"TO YOUNG GIRLS ALL OVER THE WORLD: PLEASE, BELIEVE IN YOURSELVES."
Ada Hegerberg

STAR PLAYER

CRAIG JOHNSTON

Liverpool title-winner whose futuristic boot changed the game

STAR STAT

3

years spent perfecting his boot invention

Born: 1960
Country: Australia, but born in South Africa
Position: Midfielder
Major clubs: Liverpool (England)

Key | = leader | = innovator | = scorer | = stopper

After Craig Johnston won five league titles as a midfielder for Liverpool, he invented a game-changing football boot loved by players of all levels for the way it helped them control the ball.

When he was growing up in Australia, Johnston wanted to be an architect. He would sketch out different designs for his mum's kitchen and he never lost his passion for finding solutions through design. But he also loved football. He moved across the world for a trial with English club Middlesbrough aged fifteen, his parents selling their house to raise the money for the trip. Johnston was so determined to succeed that he devised his own training programme to improve his skills. He dribbled around ten bins blindfolded and if he touched one, he would start again. Don't try this at home!

He made it into the Middlesbrough first team. In 1981, he joined Liverpool, where he was part of one of the most successful Liverpool teams in their history. He retired from football at the young age of 27, returning to Australia to look after his sister after she was injured in an accident. Family came first for him.

Johnston began coaching children and, one day, he was explaining how to swerve a ball, which can help get around the wall in a free kick. It was pouring with rain and one of the children said they couldn't do it because the boots were made of leather not table-tennis bats, which were covered in rubber pimples to help the ball swerve. Ping! Pong! Johnston had an idea!

He went home, ripped off the pimply front of a table-tennis bat and attached it to a boot with a rubber band. Immediately, the ball swerved more. He spent three years experimenting with the idea – getting through hundreds of boots – before declaring his invention ready for the game: The Predator was born.

HERE'S THE RUB

To make a ball swerve, you need to kick it so it spins as it goes forward. To make the ball spin, the boot needs to hit the ball at an angle and, during that moment of contact, the boot must rub the ball sideways as much as it can. The material on The Predator is designed to have more "rub" on the ball than a traditional boot.

The idea for The Predator boot was simple: knobbly rubber nodules on the surface of the boot improved control and made it more likely for players to hit the target. At first, boot manufacturers rejected him. But Johnston was determined and did not give up.

He went to Bayern Munich and asked three of their most famous former players – World Cup winners Franz Beckenbauer, Karl-Heinz Rummenigge and Paul Breitner – to have a kick-around wearing the boots. He filmed them playing and interviewed them talking about the boots afterwards. Johnston couldn't understand what the German players were saying but he showed Adidas the video. The sportswear maker loved it.

Adidas didn't have anywhere to test out the boot so they converted an empty swimming pool into a science laboratory and ran experiments to measure The Predator's swerve, power and accuracy. Eventually Adidas made The Predator, and players loved the better control and increased power and bend they could generate. David Beckham was wearing Predators when he scored from inside his own half for Manchester United in 1996, as was Zinédine Zidane when he helped France win the 1998 World Cup. Millions of others copied them. It made the company extremely successful – and all thanks to the Australian whose love of design never left him.

FOOTBALL'S BEST INVENTIONS

NAME	DATE	PURPOSE
Goal nets	1891	Ended arguments over whether a goal had been scored
Substitutes	1965	Allowed teams to replace injured players mid-game
Penalty shoot-out	1969	Meant that a winner could be decided if the match was a draw
Red card	1970	Showed players and fans who has been sent off
VAR	2018	Allowed contentious refereeing decisions to be checked using video

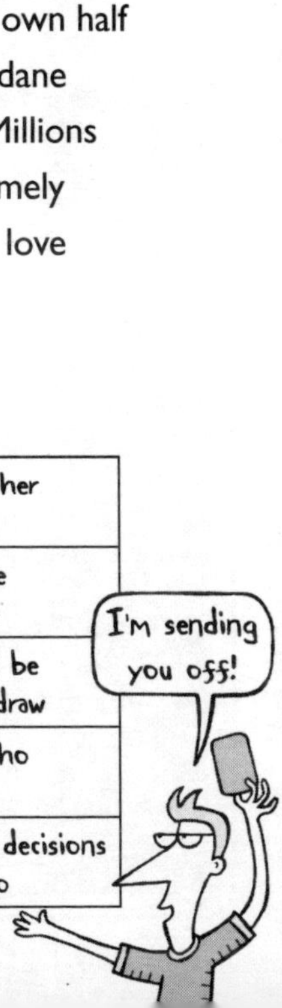

STAR PLAYER

HARRY KANE

Dedicated England captain spurred on by rejection

Born: 1993
Country: England
Position: Centre-forward
Major clubs: Tottenham Hotspur (England)
International highlights: Played in 2016 Euros; semi-finalist, 2018 World Cup
Individual awards: Winner, Golden Boot, 2018 World Cup

STAR STAT

6
goals scored in the 2018 World Cup

Key | = leader | = innovator | = scorer | = stopper

Relentless in training and prolific in front of goal, Harry Kane is the hard-working centre-forward who overcame a series of rejections to become England captain and the Golden Boot winner for scoring the most goals at the 2018 World Cup. Humble Harry is a true hero!

Kane's path to the top has been far from easy. Although he's a Tottenham Hotspur fan and grew up near their stadium, he started out at the academy of their rivals, Arsenal. But he was released when he was eight. "We'll just work harder and find another club," his dad, Pat, told him. That's exactly what Kane did – although it took time.

Kane was eleven when he joined the Spurs academy. At eighteen, he was sent on loan to clubs playing in lower divisions, like Leyton Orient, Millwall, Norwich and Leicester. He scored a handful of goals but never stood out as a star of the future. During this period, Kane wondered if he'd ever play in the Premier League. He later said that coming through these episodes of self-doubt, and developing resilience in the face of adversity, was crucial to his career success.

He was stuck on the substitutes' bench at Leicester when he watched an American football documentary that changed his mindset. Kane learned that New England Patriots quarterback, Tom Brady, was always overlooked as a youngster. Brady worked obsessively to improve and became one of the most successful players in American football history. Kane was inspired: he even called one of his dogs Brady! From that day on, he was going to be like Brady and work as hard as possible to get his chance.

His moment came in November 2014 when, after scoring a few goals for Spurs in Cup competitions, he scored his first Premier League goal with a last-minute free kick to beat Aston Villa. "All the things I went through *before* I scored Goal Number One ... that's what made me who I am," he said. Kane kept his place in the team and went on to score over 30 goals that season. A Spurs star was born.

Fans weren't quite sure why he scored so many; he was not especially fast, tall, strong or a natural dribbler. But Kane just couldn't stop scoring, and he averaged more than 34 goals over the next three seasons, joining a select group, including Alan Shearer, Wayne Rooney and Thierry Henry, with over 100 Premier League goals.

As Kane developed, it turned out that he was good at everything – scoring with either foot, holding up the ball, crossing for team-mates and heading. His main strength, though, was his drive and determination: the continued effort he put in to improve his game. He stayed late after training for extra shooting, focusing on aiming low in the corners. He became stronger and faster, took ice baths to aid his recovery, employed a chef at home to ensure his nutrition was correct and even learned to love eating fish. His dedication extended to his fans: he once spent two hours in the stadium car park signing autographs.

These are the reasons why England coach Gareth Southgate appointed him captain before the 2018 World Cup. "He is absolutely the role model you want," said Southgate. England reached the World Cup semi-final and Kane was the top scorer in the tournament with six goals, becoming only the second Englishman (after Gary Lineker in 1986) to win the Golden Boot.

GOLDEN BOOTS

Recent World Cup top scorers:

YEAR	PLAYER	GOALS
1982	Paolo Rossi (Italy)	6
1986	Gary Lineker (England)	6
1990	Salvatore Schillaci (Italy)	6
1994	Oleg Salenko (Russia) / Hristo Stoichkov (Bulgaria)	6
1998	Davor Suker (Croatia)	6
2002	Ronaldo (Brazil)	8
2006	Miroslav Klose (Germany)	5
2010	Thomas Muller (Germany)	5
2014	James Rodriguez (Colombia)	6
2018	Harry Kane (England)	6

STAR PLAYER

KATAYOUN KHOSROWYAR

Campaigner, player and coach changing the world for Muslim women

STAR STAT

Born: 1987
Country: Born in USA, played for Iran
Position: Defender/midfielder
Major clubs: Carranza FC (Spain)

30
appearances for Iran

Key | = leader | = innovator | = scorer | = stopper

Former Iran women's captain Katayoun Khosrowyar has empowered a generation of women footballers in the Middle East by making FIFA change its rules on headscarves. Khosrowyar was born in the USA and was always an avid footballer. She first visited Iran aged sixteen on a holiday to see her grandparents. She was invited to play for the national team on that trip and has never looked back.

But the path for women's football in Iran hasn't been easy.

In 2011, Khosrowyar was playing in an Olympic qualifying match when a FIFA official disqualified the team because the players were wearing hijab headscarves. The hijab is part of traditional Muslim dress, and in Iran women are required to wear them in public.

Previously, FIFA had claimed the hijab was a religious symbol, arguing that players were not allowed to make religious statements on the pitch. However, FIFA had now changed the reason, claiming the hijab was a choking hazard.

Khosrowyar set up a campaign called Let Us Play and demanded that FIFA change the rules. She was supported by high-profile figures in Asian football and the United Nations. In 2013, FIFA ruled that Muslim women are allowed to wear the hijab. (And likewise, Sikh men can wear turbans and Jewish men can wear kippah caps.) Clothing manufacturers now make sports hijabs for female athletes.

Thanks to Khosrowyar's campaign, thousands of Iranian women now play football. After captaining the Iran national team, she became the first Iranian woman to receive a FIFA coaching licence, and now coaches the Under-19 Iran team. She hopes one day to coach the senior team.

STAR PLAYER

VINCENT KOMPANY

Role-model who is a defender, leader and national symbol

Born: 1986
Country: Belgium
Position: Defender
Major clubs: Anderlecht (Belgium), Hamburg (Germany), Manchester City (England)
International highlights: Played in 2014 World Cup; semi-finalist, 2018 World Cup

STAR STAT

5
number of languages he speaks

Key | = leader | = innovator | = scorer | = stopper

Vincent Kompany is direct, intelligent and not afraid to voice his opinions. In fact, he's the captain that every club and country wants. Whether sliding in for a last-ditch challenge, or calling out injustice and holding politicians to account, he is responsible and honourable. Kompany is a global citizen – or should that be *Cityzen*! – who cares about the world and is determined to help future generations.

Kompany was born in Brussels and first played for his local side, Anderlecht, when he was seventeen. He won Belgium's player of the year award in his first season and moved to German club Hamburg at 20. After two injury-disrupted seasons, he joined Manchester City, where he became one of the most important players in the club's history.

Kompany captained Manchester City to their first four Premier League titles. His leadership shaped City, who had not won the top-division title for over 40 years. Kompany, described by the club as a "Warrior, Captain, Leader", always leads by example. His approach to wearing the armband is simple: he makes sure everyone in the team has a voice and gets the same attention. He supports team-mates and offers advice when they need it, and he calms players down if things get heated during games. He is also a fantastic ambassador for the club at home and abroad: for example, Kompany pledged to donate all the proceeds from his testimonial – a special match to mark his ten years at City (a rare achievement in modern football) – to a charity helping homeless people in Manchester.

Kompany is so multi-talented you could forget that first and foremost he is a defender; at his peak he was one of the best centre-backs in the world. He describes his position as being the "master of the castle" and his role to protect the fort, which is the goal. He has thought carefully about his game and his tips for defenders are lessons to us all:

ON WINNING A HEADER

"People try to out-jump each other ... but the only thing you have to do is fight for the spot where the ball is going to land. If you own that zone, it's going on your head, and you don't even need to jump."

ON MARKING AN OPPONENT

"Anticipate. Read his body language. Marking someone is actually just guessing where he's going."

WORKING TOGETHER

"People overestimate the importance of actually being good [individually]. The most important thing is to be a good defensive unit. I'm 60 per cent better if the guys next to me have an understanding."

As well as being a star for City, Kompany also served as Belgium captain for over eight years. During that period he became known for his intelligent comments about world affairs, including immigration, poverty and presidential elections. One journalist described him as Belgium's best foreign minister. He speaks five languages and, while in Manchester, studied Business at university.

Kompany is proud of his heritage as the son of a Belgian mother and Congolese father. "I'm not half-Belgian and half-Congolese. I am 100 per cent Belgian and 100 per cent Congolese," he said. Like many of our Star Players, Kompany uses his status to help others. He has raised funds to provide housing, medical care and education for orphans in DR Congo, and is an international ambassador for a children's charity. In Belgium, he bought a third-division football club in Brussels to offer sporting and social opportunities for disadvantaged children in his home city. Kompany has improved teams wherever he has played, and is dedicated to improving the world as well. What a star!

This is Vincent and his dad, Pierre, who moved to Belgium from the Democratic Republic of Congo as a refugee in 1975, and was elected as Belgium's first black mayor in a district of Brussels in 2018. Pierre is an engineer as well as a politican, and Kompany is very proud of him. Maybe one day Kompany will follow Papa Pierre into the world of politics!

STAR PLAYER

DIEGO MARADONA

Mischievous footballing god and World Cup hero

Born: 1960
Country: Argentina
Position: Attacking midfielder
Major clubs: Boca Juniors (Argentina), Barcelona (Spain), Napoli (Italy)
International highlights: Scored in 1982 World Cup; winner, 1986 World Cup; finalist, 1990 World Cup; scored in 1994 World Cup

STAR STAT

11

touches of the ball when scoring Goal of the Century

Key | = leader | = innovator | = scorer | = stopper

Diego Maradona scored arguably the most famous goal in football history. Certainly it was the most infamous. In the Argentina v. England quarter-final of the 1986 World Cup, he jumped for a header but instead palmed the ball with his hand and it bounced into the net. The referee didn't spot the foul and the goal was allowed. It is known as the Hand of God because Maradona joked it was scored "a little bit by the hand of God, another bit by the head of Maradona".

The goal was unforgettable because it was a blatant handball in a high-profile game scored by the best player in the world at that time. Maradona was an attacking player with huge charisma and amazing technical skills. Perhaps only someone as cunning and fearless as he was would have attempted something so audacious – and got away with it!

Maradona was brought up in a poor area of Buenos Aires, the capital of Argentina. The youth coach who spotted him aged eight was amazed he had so much talent for someone so young. He made his professional debut for Argentinos Juniors, in the top tier of the Argentine league, shortly before his sixteenth birthday, and made his debut for Argentina a few months later.

In Argentina, *pibe* is a slang term for "boy", but it is also used to describe a certain type of Argentinian footballer: short and plucky, who plays with a childlike freedom and mischief. Maradona, who is 5 feet 5 inches tall, is the greatest example of this national style. Early in his career, he earned the nickname *Pibe de Oro*, or Golden Boy.

“TO SEE THE BALL, TO RUN AFTER IT, MAKES ME THE HAPPIEST MAN IN THE WORLD.”
Diego Maradona

In 1982, Maradona moved to Europe, first to Barcelona and the following season to Napoli, both times for world-record fees. He was a superb dribbler who, despite his small stature, could shrug off challenges from big defenders. One goal he scored for Barcelona even drew applause from opposing Real Madrid fans! He was always the dominant personality in his teams, where the tactics tended to simply be "Pass it to Diego", and he helped Napoli win the Serie A title for the first time.

But his greatest moment was during the 1986 World Cup. Four minutes after he scored the Hand of God goal, he scored again: another goal full of fun and fearlessness, but this time without breaking the rules. Receiving the ball in his own half, he dribbled past five English players and dummied the keeper in a strike that won a FIFA vote for Goal of the Century. He scored both goals in the semi-final against Belgium and laid on the winning goal in the final.

Maradona won the 1986 World Cup Golden Ball for best player: perhaps in no other World Cup has a single player made such a large individual contribution to winning the title.

Maradona is idolised in Argentina as the country's greatest sporting hero. They love him not only because of his victories, but because he was a *pibe*. He always played football with the irresistible mischief of a child.

THE KING AND I

Maradona and Pelé are frequently mentioned as the two greatest players of all time. Who was best? You decide!

PELÉ	MARADONA
Scored more goals, won more World Cups, wider array of skills, more of an athlete, stayed longer at the top of his game. But did not play in a top European league.	A more effective dribbler, played in a more competitive league where he made unfancied Napoli champions, won the World Cup almost on his own. But had a wayward side, such as the Hand of God.

STAR PLAYER

MARTA

Brazil forward six times voted the world's best footballer

Born: 1986
Country: Brazil
Position: Forward
Major clubs: Umeå, Tyresö, Rosengård (all Sweden), Santos (Brazil)
International highlights: finalist, 2007 World Cup
Individual awards: Winner, 2006, 2007, 2008, 2009, 2010 and 2018 FIFA World Player of the Year

STAR STAT

5

years in a row awarded Fifa World Player of the Year

Key | = leader | = innovator | = scorer | = stopper

> "WE ALL HAVE OBSTACLES. THE FEELING OF SATISFACTION COMES BY OVERCOMING SOMETHING."
> Marta

Marta overcame huge obstacles to become one of the world's best ever female players. Although she comes from Brazil, the country of Pelé and Neymar, when Marta was growing up she faced far more challenges to play the game than any of her contemporaries in Europe or North America.

Women's football was illegal in Brazil until 1979, and a prejudice remained against it long after. Marta played kick-abouts, often the only girl in a team of boys. She faced the disapproval of her family, and there were no professional teams nearby. When she joined a club, aged fourteen, it was in Rio de Janeiro – 1,000 miles away from her home.

A lack of opportunities for women footballers in Brazil led to her moving at eighteen to Sweden, which has one of the strongest women's leagues in the world. She quickly made her mark as an attacker with great technical ability, speed, creativity and eye for goal.

Between 2006 and 2010, she won FIFA's World Player of the Year a record five times in a row. She has won seven league titles in Sweden, at three different clubs, and two league titles in the USA, at two different clubs.

In 2007, Marta led Brazil to second place in the World Cup, its best ever result. She was the tournament's top scorer and voted its best player. Marta is now the highest scorer in the Women's World Cup and her total in all matches for Brazil is well over 100 goals, making her Brazil's top scorer ever – higher even than King Pelé! Arise, Queen Marta!

STAR PLAYER

JUAN MATA

Smart midfielder using football to help others

Born: 1988
Country: Spain
Position: Attacking midfielder
Major clubs: Valencia (Spain), Chelsea, Manchester United (both England)
International highlights: Winner, 2010 World Cup; winner, 2012 Euros (scored in final)

STAR STAT

1%
of salary he gives to charity

Key | = leader | = innovator | = scorer | = stopper

Juan Mata is an intelligent midfielder. On the pitch his ability to find and create space between the midfield and attack helped Spain win the 2010 World Cup and the 2012 European Championship, and Chelsea win the Champions League. Off the pitch he likes reading books and visiting museums.

Mata wants to use football to change the world. He believes that footballers have a responsibility to think about others who haven't had the same opportunities. He founded a charitable movement, Common Goal, which encourages professional footballers and managers to donate one per cent of their salaries to projects that use football to promote education, health and peace around the world.

Professional players earn huge amounts and Mata's annual salary is believed to be around £7 million, which means he gives Common Goal about £70,000 a year. Mata's charity aims to unite the football community around the world to play for the same goal of helping others. He has persuaded over 100 other footballers to pledge one per cent of their salaries too, including Mats Hummels of Germany, Giorgio Chiellini of Italy, Shinji Kagawa of Japan, Megan Rapinoe of the USA and Alfie Mawson of England. He hopes that in the future one per cent of all the money in football will go to charitable projects. We hope he succeeds. This Mata matters!

STAR PLAYER

KYLIAN MBAPPÉ

World Cup winner in a hurry to become world's best

Born: 1998
Country: France
Position: Centre-forward
Major clubs: Monaco, Paris Saint-Germain (both France)
International highlights: Winner, 2018 World Cup (scored in final)

STAR STAT

19
age when scored in World Cup final

In his short football career, Kylian Mbappé has broken records galore and scored a famous goal to help France win the 2018 World Cup. If he goes on to fulfil his potential, he will surely become one of the best players in the world – he is already one of the fastest!

Mbappé was only nineteen when he came to global prominence during the 2018 World Cup, notably in France's 4–3 win over Lionel Messi's Argentina. Mbappé scored two goals and set up another. His incredible dribbling speed and all-round impact was symbolic: it was as though Messi, one of the world's best players, was handing over his crown to the new kid on the block, Mbappé.

Mbappé leaves his opponents trailing in his wake. In December 2017, he ran from inside his own half to score a breakaway goal for his club, Paris Saint-Germain, against Lille. His top speed was recorded at 27.7 miles per hour. That's as quick as sprinter Usain Bolt, the speediest man in the world, and Bolt didn't have a ball at his feet! One reporter wrote that Mbappé sometimes plays the game quicker than we can watch it.

Mbappé had not burst onto the scene from nowhere. His parents are both sporty: mum, Fayza, was a professional handball player and his dad, Wilfried, played for and coached their local Parisian team, AS Bondy. At two years old, Mbappé would wander into the Bondy dressing room clutching a football to listen to the team talk.

Mbappé first played for Bondy aged six and it was quickly apparent that he was special. He was small but had better technique and vision than everyone else. Even then, he was fast. Aged twelve, he moved to France's national academy in Clairefontaine and every French club wanted to sign him, as did Real Madrid, Chelsea, Manchester City, Liverpool and Bayern Munich. He decided to join Monaco, and got his first-team chance at sixteen, when he broke fellow French legend Thierry Henry's record as Monaco's youngest player.

YOUNGEST WORLD CUP FINAL GOAL-SCORERS

NAME	COUNTRY	YEAR	RESULT	AGE
Pelé	Brazil	1958	Brazil 5 Sweden 2	17 years 8 months
Kylian Mbappé	France	2018	France 4 Croatia 2	19 years 6 months
Marianne Pettersen	Norway	1995	Norway 2 Germany 0	20 years 6 months
Simone Laudehr	Germany	2007	Germany 2 Brazil 0	21 years 2 months
Wolfgang Weber	W Germany	1966	England 4 W Germany 2	22 years 1 month

The following season, Mbappé scored 26 goals to help Monaco win the 2017 French league title and reach the Champions League semi-finals. He joined Paris Saint-Germain in the summer of 2017, costing €180 million, at the time the world's second most expensive signing after Neymar.

He scored another 21 goals as PSG won the 2018 league title. Then came the World Cup and more records: he was the youngest European player to score two goals in a World Cup game, and after scoring France's final goal in their 4–2 win over Croatia, became the first teenager to score in a World Cup final since Pelé in 1958.

Those close to Mbappé say that he loves his family, respects his elders and is extremely generous; he donated his fee for winning the World Cup to a charity that helps children with disabilities play sport. And the most exciting thing about Mbappé is that his future is ahead of him.

“THE GREATEST PLAYERS ARE THE MOST HUMBLE ONES, THE ONES WHO RESPECT PEOPLE THE MOST... TO BECOME A GREAT FOOTBALL PLAYER, YOU MUST BE BEFORE ALL A GREAT MAN.”

Kylian Mbappé

STAR PLAYER

LIONEL MESSI

Goal-scoring legend who may be the best player in history

Born: 1987
Country: Argentina
Position: Forward
Major clubs: Barcelona (Spain)
International highlights: Finalist, 2007 Copa América; finalist, 2014 World Cup; finalist, 2015 Copa América; finalist, 2016 Copa América
Individual awards: Winner, 2009, 2010, 2011, 2012 and 2015 Ballon D'Or

STAR STAT

50
goals scored in a single La Liga season

Key | = leader | = innovator | = scorer | = stopper

Lionel Messi overcame a serious medical condition in childhood to become one of football's all-time greatest players. A prolific goal-scorer for club and country, the Argentinian has won the Ballon D'Or a record-equalling five times, and is the only player to have won it four years in a row.

Messi was born and brought up in Rosário, a city in central Argentina. He started playing football with his elder brothers and cousins, and aged six he joined the youth side of local club Newell's Old Boys. His youth team became near invincible, but when he was ten he faced upsetting news. His doctor diagnosed that his body wasn't creating enough of a certain hormone (important chemicals that the body needs) that would allow him to grow properly. It was unlikely he would ever become a professional footballer. The problem could be solved if he underwent treatment, but it was expensive and his family could not afford it. Newell's were unable to pay either. Only one club offered to fund the treatment: Barcelona. So Messi, aged only thirteen, left Argentina and moved to Spain, on the other side of the world.

Once he began treatment, Messi started to grow and is now 1.70m high (5ft 6ins), which is a normal adult height, if a bit shorter than average. Yet his short stature is now one of his advantages, since it allows him to be more agile than other players.

Messi is the most outstanding dribbler in the modern game, and maybe of all time. His ball control while running at speed is so impressive it looks like the ball is glued to his foot. Former Barcelona coach Pep Guardiola once said that Messi is the only person who can run faster with the ball than without it. One goal Messi scored in the 2015 Copa del Rey final against Athletic Bilbao summed this up: he ran 55 metres in 11.4 seconds, beating three defenders with three touches in the space of 1.2 seconds. His shot then flew into the net at 48 miles per hour! Don't blink when Leo plays, you might miss it!

When he made his Barcelona debut, aged seventeen, he became the club's youngest ever player and, a year later, its youngest ever goal-scorer. He gradually became the star of the team, a playmaker as well as a striker, able to make perfect passes to team-mates and score beautiful goals.

Messi doesn't just score goals – he has left his mark on the game in other ways. He has made the position of the false 9 popular. Usually the number 9 is the centre-forward closest to the opposition goal. The false 9 drops into midfield and becomes harder to mark, allowing others to run into the centre-forward's space, or timing a run to arrive in the box unmarked to score. No one has been as good a false 9 as Messi – that's the truth!

> "I DON'T CONSIDER MYSELF THE BEST, I THINK I AM JUST ANOTHER PLAYER. ON THE FIELD, WE ARE ALL THE SAME WHEN THE GAME BEGINS."
>
> Lionel Messi

In addition to helping Barcelona win many Liga, Copa del Rey and Champions League titles, he has amassed several personal records: the most goals scored in a single La Liga season, the most goals scored overall in La Liga, the most goals scored in a club football season in Europe, and the most in a calendar year. In one season, Messi's 50 league goals were more than fourteen Spanish teams had managed to score in total. It was not only the quantity of the goals that was astonishing, but the quality of them: solo dribbles, free kicks, headers, even his tap-ins at the end of passing moves were incredible!

For all his confidence and cool-headedness on the pitch, Messi is a shy and reserved man outside of football. He still keeps in touch with his team-mates from Newell's Old Boys, and he married someone he has known since he was five years old. He is also a Goodwill Ambassador for the United Nations Children's Fund and donates money to causes that help vulnerable children: he has not forgotten that he once needed medical help as a child.

STAR PLAYER

LUKA MODRIĆ

Skinny midfielder who became the perfect playmaker

Born: 1985
Country: Croatia
Position: Midfielder
Major clubs: Tottenham Hotspur (England), Real Madrid (Spain)
International highlights: Scored in 2008 Euros; scored in 2016 Euros; finalist, 2018 World Cup
Individual awards: Winner, 2018 Ballon D'Or

STAR STAT

3
World Cups he has appeared in

Key | = leader | = innovator | = scorer | = stopper

Luka Modrić was told again and again he was too skinny and small to make it. But the classy Croatian proved all his doubters wrong to become arguably the best midfielder of his generation. He has four Champions League trophies with Real Madrid and won the 2018 Ballon D'Or.

Modrić was raised by his grandfather in a small village, since his parents worked long hours at a local factory. But when he was six years old, his life changed. A war was brewing between Croatia and neighbouring Serbia. In one skirmish, a gang of Serbs killed Modrić's grandfather as he was walking his cattle through the village. The rest of the family fled and spent the next years as refugees living in a hotel on the Croatian coast.

Modrić was always a fragile-looking kid, small for his age. But he loved football and was always playing it in the hotel car park. He showed promise and went for a trial at Hajduk Split, one of the biggest clubs in Croatia and the team he supported, but they turned him down, saying he wasn't physically strong enough. Instead, aged sixteen, Modrić signed with Hajduk's rivals, Dinamo Zagreb, who when he was eighteen loaned him out to play in the notoriously tough Bosnian league. There he had to learn not to get crushed and stamped on by defenders. Because he couldn't win by force, he developed a style of play based on impeccable positioning, perfect passing and incessant movement.

"MAYBE I LOOK LIGHTWEIGHT BUT I AM A REALLY STRONG PERSON MENTALLY AND PHYSICALLY, AND I NEVER HAD ANY PROBLEMS WITH MY SIZE."

Luka Modrić

Returning to play for Dinamo, in three seasons he established himself as their best player and clubs in Europe's big leagues began to take notice, even though they worried about his small stature. Tottenham had no concerns and bought him for what was then a record fee for the club. Yet again, in his first season he came in for criticism for his size, as fans, the press and even opposition coaches wondered whether his lightweight frame could cope in the physically demanding Premier League.

Soon, however, he was thriving. Modrić became a key player at Spurs, controlling the midfield by either breaking up an attack with a timely interception, opening up the opposition defence with a quick pass, or simply keeping the ball better than anyone with his accomplished passing. After four years in England, he moved to Real Madrid, where he helped the Spanish club to win an unprecedented

four Champions League finals and he established himself as one of the most influential midfielders in the world.

In the 2018 World Cup, Modrić was the decisive player for his country, as Croatia reached the final for the first time in their history. His performances in the heart of the midfield were inspirational and he won the Golden Ball for best player of the tournament. A humble and shy man away from football, Modrić has showed that on the pitch mental strength and dedication matter more than physical build.

> A playmaker is someone in the midfield who passes the ball quickly and intelligently, and has the positional sense to intercept and break up opposition attacks. The best playmakers dominate matches as they touch the ball so often; and Modrić is one of the world's best. His quick feet allow him to slalom away from tackles, and his passes are perfectly weighted. He is a Star Playmaker!

STAR PLAYER

NADIA NADIM

Multilingual refugee scoring goals across the world

Born: 1988
Country: Born in Afghanistan, plays for Denmark
Position: Centre-forward
Major clubs: Portland Thorns (USA), Manchester City (England), Paris Saint-Germain (France)
International highlights: Finalist, 2017 Euros

STAR STAT

Aged
12
she became a refugee

Key | = leader | = innovator | = scorer | = stopper

Brought up in war-torn Afghanistan, where girls were forbidden from playing football outside their own homes, the irrepressible Nadia Nadim made an extraordinary journey to become one of the world's top centre-forwards. She has played for some of the biggest clubs in Europe and the USA, and appeared for Denmark in the 2017 European Championship final.

Nadim loved playing sport as a child, even though in Afghanistan in the late 1990s there were almost no opportunities for girls. The authority that ruled the country, the Taliban, banned women from leaving their homes unless accompanied by a male relative, and girls over the age of eight were not allowed to go to school. Nadim was only able to play football in secret with her father and four sisters in their back garden.

When Nadim was twelve, the Taliban killed her dad, who was an army general. Nadim's mum decided it was too dangerous for the family to stay in the country. They escaped to Pakistan by road, flew to Italy, and then paid strangers to smuggle them to the UK. Nadim, her mum and her sisters hid in a truck and were made to stay completely silent. Thirty hours later they jumped out and learned they had arrived ... in Denmark.

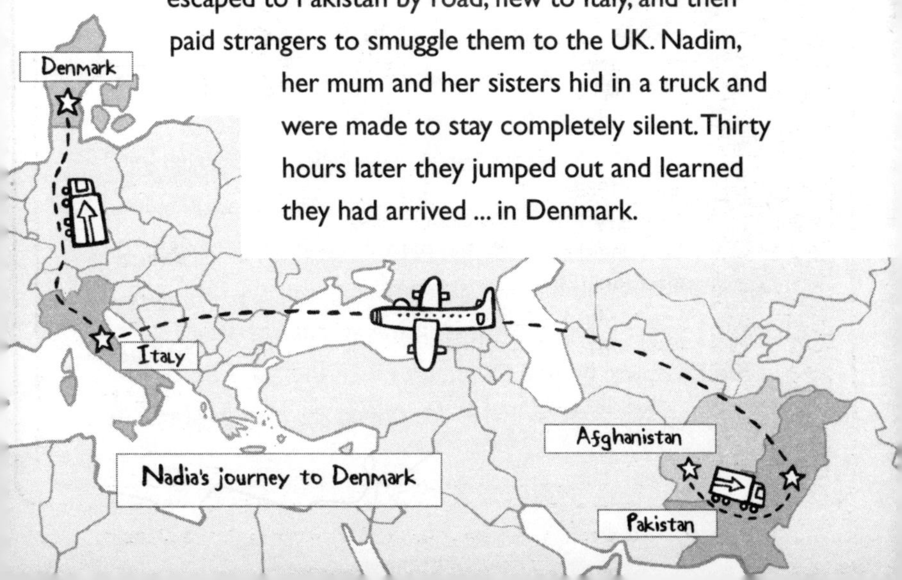

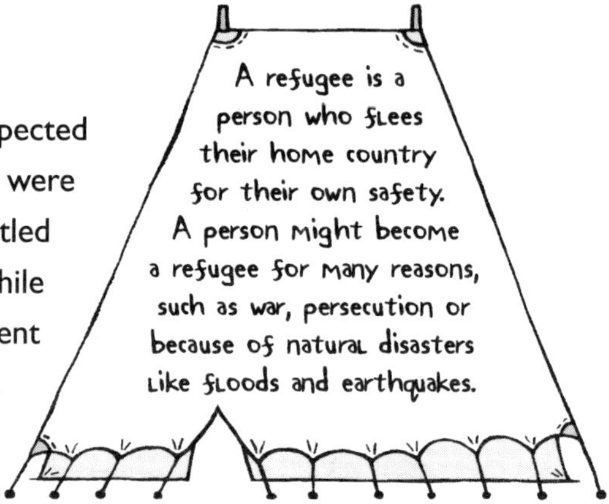

It wasn't their expected destination, but they were safe. The Nadims settled in a refugee camp, while the Danish government found them a house. The family enjoyed their new-found freedom and the girls enrolled in school. Nadim learned to speak Danish and English – and now speaks nine languages! Nadim's mum worked three jobs to earn enough money to look after the family.

Nadim was drawn to Denmark's vast green playing fields and discovered a passion for football. Soon she practised keepy-uppies whenever she could and even slept with balls in her bed. When she joined a local team, she scored three goals on her debut – even though she was playing in defence! When Nadim needed a new pair of boots, she got a job delivering newspapers from 3 a.m. to 8 a.m. every morning before school. Nothing was going to stop her from playing.

Nadim joined a professional team called IK Skovbakken. She continued to score goals and was called up to play for Denmark, as she was now officially a Danish citizen. She was confident and fearless in front of goal: she joined one of the biggest women's teams in the world, Portland Thorns in the USA, and helped Denmark reach the 2017 European Championship final. In 2018, she played for Manchester City.

Because she lacked the opportunities to play football when she was younger, Nadim is now passionate about getting girls involved in the sport. She encouraged girls in Denmark to play and, before long, had enough players to set up a local women's club with seven teams.

Nadim also loves helping people and when she stops playing football, she wants to become a reconstructive surgeon, rebuilding parts of patients' bodies that have been affected by accidents or disease.

Nadim has an infectious enthusiasm for everything she does. Her family called it The Nadi Effect. "It's about getting people together, making them feel comfortable, having fun and making people laugh," she told us. "But most of all, it's about me being me."

> "MY STORY SHOWS THAT NO MATTER WHERE YOU COME FROM OR WHAT YOU'VE BEEN THROUGH, ANYTHING IS POSSIBLE."
>
> Nadia Nadim

STAR PLAYER

MANUEL NEUER

World Cup winner who reinvented the goalkeeper position

Born: 1986
Country: Germany
Position: Goalkeeper
Major clubs: Schalke 04, Bayern Munich (both Germany)
International highlights: Winner, 2014 World Cup

STAR STAT

21

touches of the ball outside his area in a World Cup game, a record

Key | = leader | = innovator | = scorer | = stopper

Germany has a long tradition of producing great goalkeepers, and Manuel Neuer might just be the best ever. He helped Germany win the 2014 World Cup and has changed the way many modern goalkeepers approach their role.

Neuer always had strong arms. When he was young, he excelled at throwing balls into faraway targets in training sessions. In one of his first matches as a professional, he threw the ball from his own area, almost the length of the whole pitch, to set up a goal. It was his first assist!

"I'M STANDING FOR SECURITY AND PROTECTION, AND YOU HAVE TO GIVE YOUR TEAM-MATES THAT FEELING AS WELL."

Manuel Neuer

Neuer has the tools that all great goalkeepers need: bravery, confidence, anticipation, technical ability, peripheral vision and fast reflexes. He is also smart. And that intelligence has helped him reinvent the role of the modern goalkeeper. In the past, the job of a goalkeeper was simple: to stop goals going in by catching crosses and making saves. Neuer has created a new task list for goalkeepers. He uses his position to organize the defence, disrupt attacks outside the penalty-area and start his own team's attacks. Neuer is as good with his feet as with his hands. Coach Joachim Löw, who appointed Neuer as Germany captain in 2016, said he was good enough to play in midfield and, as a result, is involved in all aspects of his team's play.

Most goalkeepers tend to only touch the ball inside their own penalty area: Neuer showed his genius in a 2014 World Cup victory against Algeria, when he made five clearances and touched the ball 21 times outside the area – a World Cup record. The tactics may have looked risky but Neuer's innovative approach allowed team-mates to play higher up the pitch, closer to the opponent's goal.

This brave style of goalkeeping has been given a name: the Sweeper Keeper. The sweeper used to play behind the defensive line, cleaning up (or sweeping) defenders' mistakes and breaking upfield to start attacks.

By positioning himself on the edge of his area, Neuer is essentially playing in two positions at the same time: the sweeper and the keeper! One Bundesliga team-mate said Neuer was so important that he made up 50 per cent of the team – not quite the right maths but it shows how highly he is valued.

Neuer's skills have been rewarded with an impressive haul of trophies, including five titles in 2013 as Bayern Munich won the German league and Cup, the Champions League, the UEFA Super Cup and the Club World Cup. Neuer also took the Golden Glove award for the best goalkeeper, after helping Germany win the 2014 World Cup. You can be sure he didn't drop any of those trophies!

STAR PLAYER

NEYMAR

☆ Super-creative forward who is vying for title of world's best player ☆

Born: 1992
Country: Brazil
Position: Forward
Major clubs: Santos (Brazil), Barcelona (Spain), Paris Saint-Germain (France)
International highlights: Semi-finalist, 2014 World Cup; scored in 2018 World Cup
Individual highlights: Winner, 2011 Puskás Award

STAR STAT

€222 MILLION transfer fee paid by Paris Saint-Germain in 2017

Key | = leader | = innovator | = scorer | = stopper

Ever since he made his professional debut aged seventeen, Neymar has displayed a cheeky flamboyance in everything he does. He loves to be creative on the pitch, taunting defenders with an amazing range of dribbles, tricks and feints. He's also a prolific goal-scorer both for his clubs and the Brazilian national team. When Paris Saint-Germain bought him in 2017, he became the most expensive player in the world – by a country mile! His price tag of €222 million (£200 million) was more than double that of the second most expensive player at the time.

Neymar's dad was a footballer who played for small Brazilian clubs but got injured and, when Neymar was a toddler, the family moved to live in a poor neighbourhood, where his mum, dad, Neymar and his sister all shared the same room. Neymar spent most of his childhood playing football on the city streets and honed his talents from a young age. Brazil fell in love with Neymar as soon as he started at Santos, his first club, because he played with unbelievable technique and an attacking, happy-go-lucky energy that reminded them of players like Pelé. In 2011, still aged only 19, he won FIFA's Puskás Award for the most beautiful goal of the year. In a game in the Brazilian league, he dribbled past two players, played a one-two with a team-mate, then dribbled past another two before beating the keeper.

In 2013, Neymar moved to Barcelona, to play alongside Lionel Messi. In his second season at Barça his attacking partnership with Messi and Luis Suárez netted 122 goals, the most in Spanish league history, and the club won the treble: La Liga, the Copa del Rey and the Champions League. That year Neymar was third in FIFA's Ballon D'Or for the best player in the world, behind Messi and Cristiano Ronaldo.

He was third in line for the Ballon D'Or again in 2017, behind the same two players. Neymar, however, is five years younger than Messi, and seven years younger than Ronaldo, so might have his best years still to come. Paris Saint-Germain were certainly thinking about his potential as world number one when they bought him for such a lot of money. In his first season in Paris, he scored almost a goal a game as they coasted to the league title.

Neymar has been Brazil's best player since he was a teenager, and since then the team has been organised around him. He was Brazil's star player in both the 2014 and 2018 World Cups. In 2018, he was the player who had the most shots on goal in the entire tournament.

Neymar has never been afraid to stand out. His hairstyles are always a subject of conversation – from the extravagant blond Mohican he wore as a youngster at Santos to the spaghetti-curls he revealed at the 2018 World Cup.

He's also a bit of a show off, whether delighting fans with an amazing rainbow flick, scoring a goal with a bicycle kick or taking selfies for his millions of fans on social media. However, he often gets attention for diving. Critics accuse him of falling over too easily, although his fans say he is shamelessly fouled because he is so good.

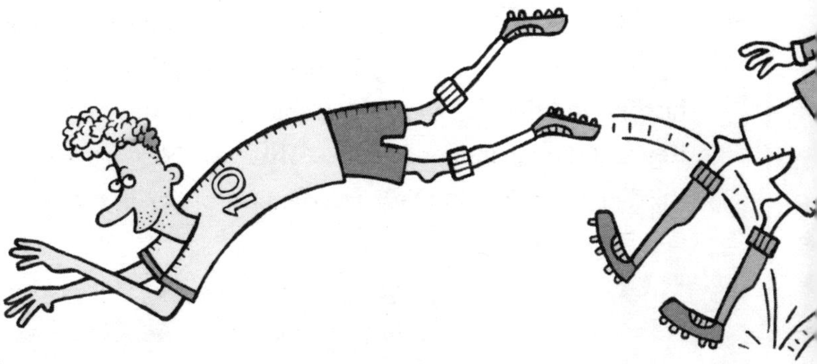

As Messi and Ronaldo approach the twilight of their careers, if Neymar can keep his focus on his game, he is well-positioned to one day inherit the title of best in the world.

STAR PLAYER

LILY PARR

Prolific goal-scorer and trailblazer for women's football

Born: 1905
Died: 1978
Country: England
Position: Forward
Major clubs: Dick, Kerr's Ladies, Preston Ladies (both England)
International highlights: Played in first ever women's international match

STAR STAT

43
goals scored in her first season, aged 14

Key | = leader | = innovator | = scorer | = stopper

Lily Parr was the world's first female football star. An intimidating goal-scorer with a ferocious left foot, she blazed a trail for women's football at a time when the sport was almost exclusively played by men. In 2002, she became the first woman to be inaugurated into the English Football Hall of Fame.

Parr was one of seven children and she grew up playing football and rugby with her older brothers in St Helens, near Liverpool. Soon she was as good as them and in 1919, aged only fourteen, she joined her local side, St Helens Ladies. In her second match she played against Dick, Kerr's Ladies, then the best women's club in England. The Dick, Kerr's coach was so impressed that he invited Parr to join the team.

Dick, Kerr was the name of a factory in Preston which, two years earlier, had founded one of the first women's teams in England. During the First World War, women had taken jobs in factories while the men went off to fight. The Dick, Kerr women's team quickly became successful, with their matches attracting thousands of spectators.

Parr moved to Preston in 1919 to work at the Dick, Kerr factory and play for its team. In her first season, still aged fourteen, she scored 43 goals. She was 6 feet tall, strong, competitive and known for a blistering shot – according to one story, she broke a male goalkeeper's arm when he tried to block one of her shots.

In 1920, tens of thousands of fans watched Dick, Kerr's play four games against a team representing France, the first ever international tournament in women's football. The attention from newspapers was turning Parr, the best player in the team, into a national hero. The following year she established her supremacy as the most devastating goal-scorer in the women's game when she scored five goals in a 9–1 defeat of a Best of Britain side, and all the goals in a 5–1 rout of the French national team.

Although women's football was attracting huge crowds, its popularity was short-lived. In 1921, the FA banned women's teams from playing on FA-affiliated pitches, saying that football was "unsuitable" for women. But really, the FA didn't like that women's success was diverting attention from the men's league, which had restarted after the war.

Dick, Kerr's carried on despite the ban, even though the crowds were much smaller. One thing didn't change: Parr kept on scoring. When the Dick, Kerr factory was sold, the team renamed themselves Preston Ladies, and continued to dominate English women's football. After leaving the factory, Parr worked as a nurse at a psychiatric hospital near Preston. She played her final game for Preston Ladies in 1950, aged 45. It is estimated that she scored more than 900 goals during her career.

Parr lived to see the FA finally lift the ban on women's football playing on affiliated pitches in 1971, and the women's game began to grow again. When the Hall of Fame was launched in 2002, Lily Parr was the only woman in the 29 names on the list. No one was on a par with Lily Parr!

STAR PLAYER

PELÉ

All-time legend who scored more goals than anyone else

Born: 1940
Country: Brazil
Position: Attacking midfielder
Major clubs: Santos (Brazil), New York Cosmos (USA)
International highlights: Winner, 1958 World Cup (scored in final); finalist, 1959 Copa América; winner, 1962 World Cup; winner, 1970 World Cup (scored in final)

STAR STAT

1,282
total goals scored in his career

Key | = leader | = innovator | = scorer | = stopper

Edson Arantes do Nascimento was born in a small town in a remote part of Brazil. By his twentieth birthday he was the most famous sportsman in the world. Perhaps no athlete in history has gone from such obscure beginnings to global stardom in such a short amount of time.

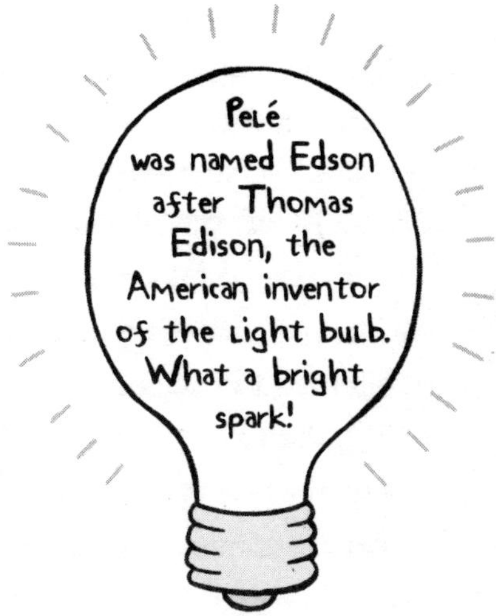

For much of his childhood, home was a small wooden house with a leaky roof, and entertainment was playing football barefoot outside with a ball made from socks. But the scrawny, competitive boy nicknamed Pelé – the word has no meaning and even he can't be sure where it came from and why it caught on – was soon getting noticed for the skill he showed with his feet.

Aged fifteen, in 1956, he signed with Santos, one of Brazil's top clubs, three hundred miles away from his home. His performances were so good that within a year he was called up for Brazil, and the following year he represented his country at the 1958 World Cup.

Pelé was the youngest player in the tournament, but this did not faze him. The skinny teenager dazzled the crowds from the off, hitting the woodwork within minutes in his first game. He played with mesmerising skill, in the same energetic, playful style of the street football he played as a child. He scored six goals in four games, including in the final, which gave Brazil its first World Cup victory. He remains the youngest person to score in a World Cup. He became known as the King, an international celebrity who was on the cover of magazines around the world. But it didn't change his life. He continued living in a house with his team-mates in Santos, where he wasn't even their best-paid player!

Pelé's impressive teenage achievements were just the start. He worked hard to develop into one of the very finest players in football history. An attacking midfielder, he had unbelievable technique and was extremely nimble, confusing opponents with his changes of direction. He was not tall, only 1.8m (5ft 8ins), but could jump higher than many taller players.

He remained down to earth, in part because back then footballers did not earn as much money as they do now, but also because he did not forget his childhood. In 1969, when he became the first – and still the only – player to score a thousand goals, he used the achievement to make a passionate call for Brazil's disadvantaged children: "Think about the poor little children, the ones who need clothes and food," he said moments after he scored the goal.

Pelé was part of the Brazil squad that won the 1962 and 1970 World Cups, making him the only player with three World Cup titles. He refused to sign with any European team and stayed at Santos for his whole career, apart from when he came out of retirement to play in the USA. Yet such was the interest across the globe in seeing Pelé play, that Santos toured many other countries to play exhibition games. When the team arrived, fans lined the streets – everyone wanted to get a glimpse of Pelé.

PELÉ IN NUMBERS

Total goals: 1282
Total games: 1367
Goals excluding exhibition games: 757
World Cups: 3
Shirt number: 10

It has been many years since Pelé retired, but his reputation is as strong as ever. In 1999, the International Olympic Committee elected him the Athlete of the Century. Even Cristiano Ronaldo says he is the best: "Pelé is the greatest player in football history," he said. "There will only be one Pelé."

"SUCCESS DOESN'T COME BY CHANCE. IT COMES FROM HARD WORK, PERSEVERANCE, LEARNING, STUDY, AND, ABOVE ALL, LOVE FOR WHAT YOU ARE DOING OR LEARNING TO DO."

Pelé

STAR PLAYER

FERENC PUSKÁS

Hungarian forward who broke scoring records at home and abroad

Born: 1927
Died: 2006
Country: Hungary
Position: Forward
Major clubs: Honvéd (Hungary), Real Madrid (Spain)
International highlights: Finalist, 1954 World Cup (for Hungary); played in 1962 World Cup (for Spain)

STAR STAT

83

goals scored for Hungary in 84 games

Key | = leader | = innovator | = scorer | = stopper

> "I WILL WRITE OF MY LIFE AS A FOOTBALLER AS IF IT WERE A LOVE STORY, FOR WHO SHALL SAY THAT IT IS NOT?"
>
> Ferenc Puskás

The charismatic Ferenc Puskás had two outstanding football careers with an eighteen-month break in between. First, he was a local hero who captained Hungary to a World Cup final. Second, he was a foreign superstar whose goals turned Real Madrid into a global phenomenon. Both careers were lit up by defining performances in key games: Hungary beating England 6–3, and Real Madrid winning the 1960 European Cup final 7–3.

Puskás was born just outside the Hungary capital of Budapest. His father was a footballer and coach. Young Puskás inherited his father's love for the game; he practised keepy-uppies with a tennis ball and played spontaneous games in the street with friends. He made his debut aged sixteen for local side Kispest, for whom he went on to score 357 goals in 354 games.

In 1949, the Hungarian government turned Kispest into the team representing the Hungarian army and changed its name to Honvéd, meaning "defender of the homeland". Every player was given a military rank and Puskás was named major. He became known as *Öcsi*, or Kid, because he was only eighteen when he made his Hungary debut.

Puskás played as a left-sided forward. He was so brilliant with his left foot that he shrugged off criticism for not using his right foot. "You can only kick with one foot at a time," he said, "otherwise you fall on your bottom." In 1953,

Hungary was the first non-British team to beat England at Wembley, winning 6–3. Shortly after, they beat them again, winning 7–1 in Hungary. Although he had never served in the army, he quickly got the nickname The Galloping Major. England captain Billy Wright declared Hungary "the best team in the world", but they lost the 1954 World Cup final to West Germany, after Puskás was injured early in the tournament. Puskás scored 83 goals in 84 Hungary games.

In 1956, Puskás's career took a decisive turn. While Honvéd was in Bilbao for a European Cup tie, a revolution broke out in Hungary in protest at the way the government ran the country. Puskás refused to return home and, as a result, he was exiled from the country and the government banned him from playing football for eighteen months.

By the time he was able to play again, he was 31 and 18 kilogrammes overweight. That didn't stop Real Madrid from signing him – and it proved a tremendous decision. Puskás scored 242 goals in 262 games for the Spanish giants. He won five league titles, was Spanish top scorer four times, and won three European Cup finals. The most dramatic came in 1960, when Puskás scored four goals as Real Madrid smashed Eintracht Frankfurt 7–3 in front of over 120,000 fans.

Puskás, who captained Hungary during its period of glory, was also a fantastic team player. He was funny and generous and he understood how to get the best out of his team-mates. He often set up goals for his Madrid strike partner Alfredo di Stéfano when he could have scored himself. He is equally loved in Hungary and Madrid and with good reason. His technique, goal record, team ethic and success over two distinct careers are why Puskás is regarded as one of the greatest European footballers of all time.

STAR PLAYER

MEGAN RAPINOE

Skilful winger, fearless leader and social activist

STAR STATS

Born: 1985
Country: USA
Position: Winger
Major clubs: Lyon (France), Seattle Reign (USA)
International highlights: Finalist, 2011 World Cup; winner, 2015 World Cup

6
games started in 2015 World Cup

Key | = leader | = innovator | = scorer | = stopper

Megan Rapinoe stands up for what she believes in – or rather, she kneels for it. The winger, who was part of the USA team that won the 2015 Women's World Cup, knelt during the American national anthem to protest against racial injustice in her country. She was acting to support American footballer Colin Kaepernick, who was the first to "take a knee" during an anthem rather than stand.

Although some criticised Rapinoe for her stance, she never backed down. She believes that her platform as a World Cup winner gives her a responsibility to spread her message of tolerance and equality. Her approach to the world is simple: "Be kind, be authentic, and help others do the same."

As a player, Rapinoe was capable of moments of genius. She was the first player in Olympic history to score a goal direct from a corner in the 2012 semi-final against Canada. She also scored in USA's opening match on its way to winning the 2015 World Cup.

Rapinoe's legacy is to be on the right side of history. She is fearless in her beliefs: standing up for gay rights and criticising sports organisations, including her bosses at US Soccer, for wage discrimination. She and her girlfriend, a professional basketball player, were the first gay couple to appear on the cover of an American sports magazine.

Rapinoe is part of Juan Mata's Common Goal movement and has set up the Rapinoe fashion label with her twin sister, Rachael. Their slogan is Be Your Best You – which is appropriate, as this Megan is the best Megan we know!

STAR PLAYER

CYRILLE REGIS

Centre-forward who inspired a generation of black footballers

Born: 1958
Died: 2018
Country: England
Position: Centre-forward
Major clubs: West Bromwich Albion, Coventry City, Aston Villa (all England)

STAR STAT

241
appearances for West Bromwich Albion

Key | = leader | = innovator | = scorer | = stopper

Cyrille Regis, a powerful centre-forward with a fearsome shot and a ready smile, was among the first black players to star in English football. Throughout his career he remained dignified and determined in the face of open racism.

Regis was born in French Guiana in South America. His family moved to England when Regis was five. Once he left school, Regis trained as an electrician, playing park football before a West Bromwich Albion scout spotted him. In 1977, he was signed, aged nineteen, and made an immediate impact in the First Division, scoring twice on his West Brom debut.

Football today includes players from all races and backgrounds but, back then, West Brom – one of the most exciting teams in England – were unique as the only club to field three black players (the other two were Laurie Cunningham and Brendon Batson). Their matches were often marred by disgusting chants from opposition fans attacking them for the colour of their skin.

Regis never let this racist abuse affect the way he played on the pitch and said it actually spurred him on to keep scoring. He always kept his cool. His goals earned him five England caps, and one stunning effort against Norwich won Goal of the Season in 1982. He helped Coventry win the 1987 FA Cup final, his only trophy. Regis was awarded an MBE for his charity work. He was a true king of the game.

STAR PLAYER

ROSE REILLY

World Cup winner who was a trailblazer for the women's game

Born: 1955
Country: Born in Scotland, played for Italy
Position: Forward
Major clubs: Reims (France), Lecce, AC Milan (both Italy)
International highlights: Winner, 1984 Mundialito Femminile (for Italy)

STAR STAT

8

League titles won in Italy

Key | = leader | = innovator | = scorer | = stopper

Rose Reilly is the only Scottish footballer to win a World Cup. She also won two league titles in two different countries playing for two different teams – in the same season. Women's football was banned in the UK during her playing career, but that didn't stop her. This Rose was a proud and fierce thistle!

Reilly spent her whole career proving people wrong. When she was seven, she gave herself a short haircut and called herself Ross so she could play in a boys' team. A scout from Glasgow club Celtic saw her score seven goals in a game and wanted to sign her – until he discovered Ross was actually Rose! She kept playing throughout the 1960s, but despite her talents it was hard for her to play professionally as the FA had banned women from playing at major grounds. She played for amateur side Stewarton Thistle, the first women's football team in Scotland, and helped them win the Scottish Cup in 1971.

Scotland kept the ban in place for a further three years until 1974, which meant Reilly was unable to play for any major women's club side. The FA ban encouraged Reilly to move to France and play for Stade de Reims. Reilly and her friend Edna Cook, a former team-mate at Stewarton, helped Reims win the 1973 league title in their first season together. The next season, they joined Italian side AC Milan and won the league again.

Reilly made a name for herself in Italy, where she taught herself three new words every day by reading the sports newspapers. She won EIGHT league titles during her time in Italy and won the top-scorer award four times.

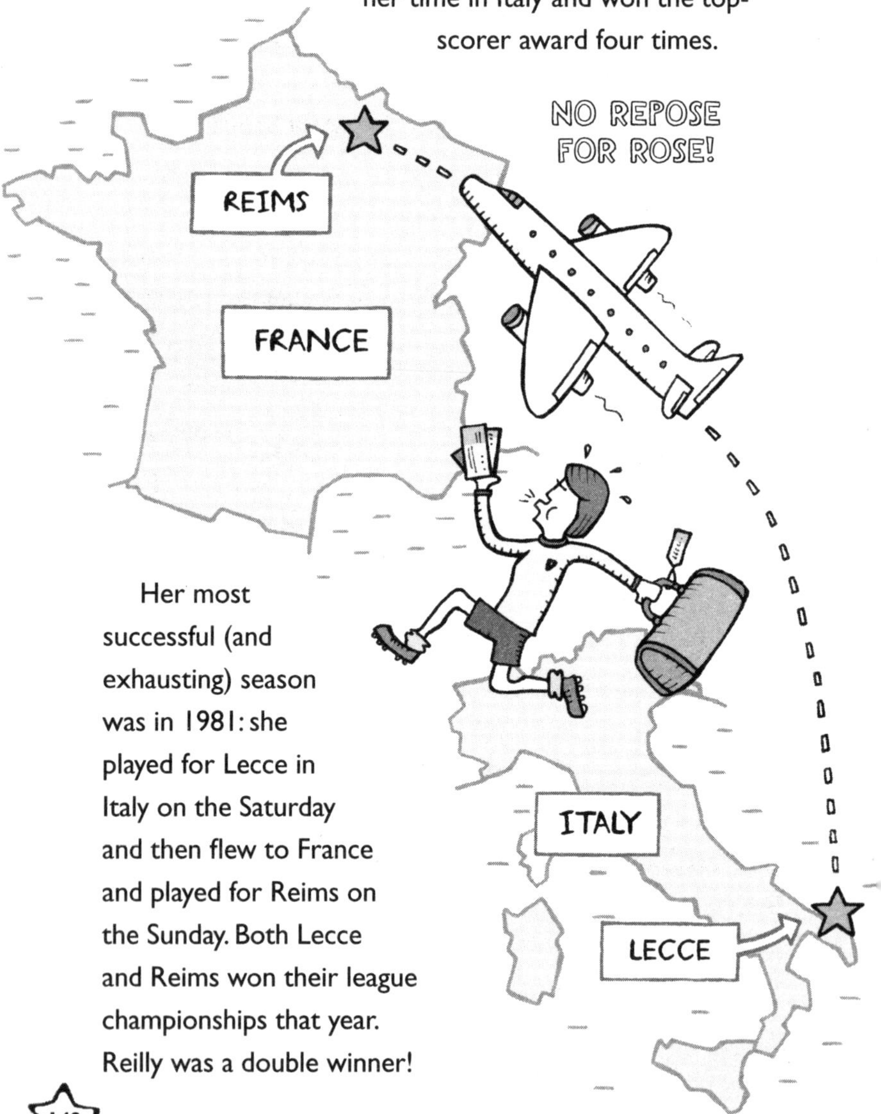

Her most successful (and exhausting) season was in 1981: she played for Lecce in Italy on the Saturday and then flew to France and played for Reims on the Sunday. Both Lecce and Reims won their league championships that year. Reilly was a double winner!

Reilly had played for Scotland in their first official game in 1972 (even though clubs were still banned from hosting women's matches), a 3–2 defeat to England. But after she criticised Scottish officials for ignoring the women's game, she was banned from ever playing for her national side again. Scotland's loss was Italy's gain: she was asked to play for Italy and so she did. "I wasn't playing for Scotland, so why not?" she said.

In the 1980s, the women's game organised a competition called Mundialito Femminile. It was a version of the Women's World Cup before FIFA organised its first official competition in 1991. Reilly played for Italy in the 1984 tournament and scored in the final, a 3–1 win over Germany. Even though Reilly celebrated with her team-mates, she admitted: "There was always a Scottish heart beating under the Italian jersey."

It took a long time for Reilly's achievements to be recognized in Scotland. She retired from football when she was 40, and eleven years later she was voted into the Scottish Football Hall of Fame. Now she is celebrated for her determination and the way she ignored all the obstacles in her path to follow her dream.

"I WAS SO IN LOVE WITH THE GAME, ALL I EVER WANTED TO DO WAS PLAY."

Rose Reilly

STAR PLAYER

JULES RIMET

Father of the World Cup

Born: 1873
Died: 1956
Country: France
Position: Founder of FIFA
International highlights: Organised first ever World Cup, 1930
Individual prizes: The original World Cup trophy is named after him

STAR STAT

13
national teams in the first World Cup

Key | = leader | = innovator | = scorer | = stopper

Frenchman Jules Rimet is the only Star Player never to have been a player at all. But we wanted to include him because he is the original World Cup hero. The tournament exists today thanks to his hard work and love of the game.

When Rimet was a young man in Paris, he and some friends started a sports club called Red Star. Of all the sports that Red Star offered, Rimet liked football best. He became active in football administration, and in 1904 he was one of the people who set up football's international federation, FIFA.

During the First World War, Rimet served as a soldier in the French army. He saw the devastation on the battlefields first hand. He became determined that once the war was over he would try to use football to solve the world's problems.

The way to achieve this dream, he thought, was to organise a tournament that would bring nations together. Rimet became FIFA president and got its members to agree to have the first World Cup in 1930, in Uruguay in South America.

The first World Cup was a brilliant success and FIFA have never looked back. In 1946, FIFA decided to honour the father of the World Cup by changing the name of the trophy to the Jules Rimet Trophy. (It was given to Brazil for keeps in 1970 when they won it for the third time.) His name is now inseparable from the competition he worked so hard to create. Hooray, Rimet!

STAR PLAYER

RONALDO

Brilliant finisher who went from zero to hero on the biggest stage of all

Born: 1976
Country: Brazil
Position: Centre-forward
Major clubs: Cruzeiro (Brazil), Barcelona, Real Madrid (both Spain), Inter Milan, AC Milan (both Italy)
International highlights: Winner, 1997 and 1999 Copa América; finalist, 1998 World Cup; winner, 2002 World Cup
Individual awards: Winner, 1997, 2002 Ballon D'Or; Golden Shoe winner, 2002 World Cup

STAR STAT

8

goals scored in 2002 World Cup

Key | = leader | = innovator | = scorer | = stopper

Before Cristiano Ronaldo, there was another Ronaldo. This Ronaldo was from Brazil and, like his Portuguese namesake, he was also for a time the best player in the world. Fast and powerful, the Brazilian Ronaldo was known for terrorising defences with short bursts of acceleration, skilful dribbles and clinical finishing. He also made one of the most remarkable comebacks in international football.

By the time Ronaldo was aged 21, in 1998, he had become the world's most expensive player twice: once when he went from PSV Eindhoven in the Netherlands to Barcelona, and then again when he transferred from Barcelona to Inter Milan. He was also the star of the Brazilian national team who were preparing for the 1998 World Cup in France.

Brazil were favourites to win the tournament, and thanks to Ronaldo's four goals and three assists they made the final. But on the day of that final, in which Brazil played France, disaster struck.

WRONG RON?

Ronaldo's nickname was O Fenómeno, or The Phenomenon, which helped distinguish him from other Ronaldos.

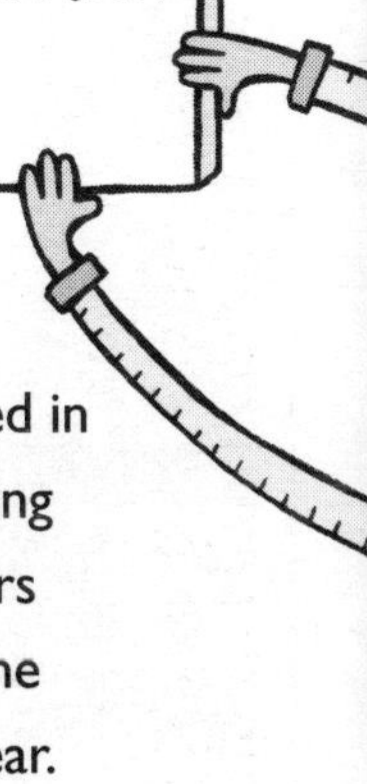

A few hours before the game, while lying on his bed in the team's hotel, Ronaldo started squirming and shaking uncontrollably. He was having some kind of fit. Doctors rushed him to a medical clinic. However, by the time he arrived, he was feeling better and was given the all-clear. Ronaldo insisted that he play in the final. But because of those disrupting few hours, Ronaldo's performance in the game was way below his normal standard, and Brazil lost 3–0. It was the biggest game of his life and it turned into a humiliation.

After the World Cup, Ronaldo returned to Inter Milan, but suffered another setback. In 1999, he ruptured a tendon in his knee during a league game, which kept him out for four months. Only seven minutes into his return game he injured the same knee – and this time he was out for more than a year.

Many fans thought Ronaldo would never play again. His strong and quick playing style and constant acceleration put huge stress on his knees. As he got older and bulkier, would his knees ever properly recover? His career appeared to be over at just 23. But Ronaldo wasn't going to be beaten.

A quiet and determined man, he showed huge physical and mental courage to work on his recuperation. He trained alone, taking

care not to rush, and maintained his self-belief even when others doubted him. His dream was to play in the 2002 World Cup in Japan and South Korea, but he missed Brazil's entire qualification campaign and it looked like he might not be ready in time. He returned to club football a few months before the 2002 World Cup. He was a last-minute selection for Brazil's squad, where he played alongside Ronaldinho and Rivaldo, a forward line known as the Three Rs.

With all Three Rs on form, Brazil cruised to the final. This time, Ronaldo was the undisputed star of the show. He scored both goals in the 2–0 victory against Germany, won the award for Man of the Match and ended the tournament with the Golden Shoe for top scorer.

Most people only get one chance at appearing in a World Cup final. Because of his determination, Ronaldo got two. He was able to rewrite his own history by coming back from the heartbreak of 1998 to become the hero of 2002.

STAR PLAYER

JAIYAH SAELUA

Transgender defender making a stand against discrimination

Born: 1988
Country: American Samoa
Position: Defender

STAR STAT

11

appearances for American Samoa national team

Key | = leader | = innovator | = scorer | = stopper

Jaiyah Saelua is the first transgender footballer to play in a World Cup qualifying match. She plays for the male national team of American Samoa, a group of five islands in the Pacific Ocean with a population of 60,000, which is one of the smallest of FIFA's 211 member countries.

Saelua was born a boy called Johnny. But she didn't feel that she was a boy – she felt that she was a girl. In American Samoa, boys who feel they are girls are known as *fa'afafine*. (In the UK, we use the word "transgender" to describe those who feel that their gender at birth does not match who they are.) In American Samoa, the *fa'afafine* are an ancient, accepted and respected group in Samoan society. Saelua liked playing football, and being a *fa'afafine* was no barrier to being chosen to play for the men's national side.

American Samoa are one of the weakest international teams and once lost a World Cup qualifier to Australia by a world-record 31–0. In fact, the team had never won an international until 2011, when with Saelua in the side, they beat Tonga 2–1. Saelua was the hero of the day, making a last-minute goal-line clearance.

Before her success playing for Samoa, Saelua studied at university in America. There she tried to play for a men's football team but was not allowed. Ever since then, Saelua has become a dedicated and inspiring ambassador for transgender athletes, fighting for the same acceptance from the world that she always had in her home country.

"ANYBODY WHO FEELS DIFFERENT IN THEIR SOCIETY OR COMMUNITY: GO OUT AND DON'T LET ANYBODY STOP YOU FROM CHASING AFTER YOUR DREAMS."

Jaiyah Saelua

STAR PLAYER

MO SALAH

Smiling goal-scorer who stays true to himself and his religion

Born: 1992
Country: Egypt
Position: Forward
Major clubs: Roma (Italy), Liverpool (England)
International highlights: Finalist, 2017 Africa Cup of Nations; scored in 2018 World Cup
Individual awards: Winner, 2018 Puskás Award

STAR STAT

More than **1 million** Egyptians voted for him in an election

Key | = leader | = innovator | = scorer | = stopper

Super striker Mo (short for Mohamed) Salah is loved by all football fans – not just ones in Egypt, where he comes from. He plays with a smile on his face, as he dribbles past his opponents to score lots of goals. Fans see that he works hard, stays humble and is true to himself.

Salah grew up in a small village called Nagrig. At fourteen years old, he started playing for his first club, Arab Contractors, which was in Egypt's capital city, Cairo, 130 kilometres away. Salah got up early to go to school, then took a four-hour bus ride to football training and then spent four hours getting home. Sometimes he returned well after midnight. For two months, he made the same journey but was stuck on the bench. He was upset not to be playing and, in tears, told his dad that he couldn't do it any more. His dad told him to keep going and train harder. Salah remembers that conversation as the moment that changed his life.

Salah's rise to the very top was down to the sacrifice, hard work and humility that he has shown since that day. He stayed behind after training to practise his finishing. He spent extra time in the gym to improve his upper-body strength. He asked his coaches how to improve his ball protection in tight spaces. His changes of direction at speed now leave defenders sprawling. His calmness in front of the goal – added to the constant improvement in the quality of his finishing – has helped increase his goal return.

> "I WORK ON THE WEAKNESSES AND TRY TO IMPROVE ALL THE TIME. EVERY YEAR I FEEL I'VE IMPROVED. THAT'S THE MOST IMPORTANT THING FOR ME."
> Mo Salah

Salah is proud to be a Muslim. When he scores for his club, he celebrates his goals in the same way as he does in Egypt: pointing his fingers up to the sky to thank God, then kneeling in a show of his faith. When Salah did this at Liverpool's Anfield Stadium, the crowd went a little quieter, as if showing respect for his religion. When he got up, the cheers grew louder again. Salah does not hide his faith and for this he is admired by many.

Salah's kneeling position after scoring goals is called *sujud*, which in Arabic means to bow down and praise God. It involves the toes, knees, hands, nose and forehead all touching the ground together.

Islam, the religion practised by Muslims, is the world's second-largest religion. Nearly one quarter of the world's population are Muslim. Other Muslim players with Premier League experience include N'Golo Kanté, Riyad Mahrez, Sadio Mané, Mesut Özil and Paul Pogba.

He's certainly a hero in Egypt. The British Museum in London included Salah's green football boots as part of its Modern Egypt exhibition. Saudi Arabia gave Salah a piece of land in Mecca, the city in Saudi Arabia that's considered to be Islam's holiest site, in recognition of his role as an inspiration to Muslims all over the world. And when Egypt's presidential election took place in 2018, over one million Egyptians voted for Salah – and his name was not even on the ballot paper!

Salah often returns home to Nagrig and is happy to help his village: he has given money to the local hospital, and paid for the renovations of a public sports centre, a school and a mosque.

He has shown young people that if you work hard and prove yourself, you will gain respect and admiration. Salah's faith has helped him on that journey. He is now inspiring millions more around the world.

STAR PLAYER

RAHEEM STERLING

Skilful winger who overcame hardship to play for England

Born: 1994
Country: England
Position: Winger
Major clubs: Liverpool, Manchester City (both England)
International highlights: Played in 2014 World Cup; semi-finalist, 2018 World Cup

STAR STAT

5 a.m.
time he got up to help his mum work

Key | = leader | = innovator | = scorer | = stopper

For winger Raheem Sterling, playing at Wembley is like playing at home. Literally! He grew up almost next door to the stadium. Its famous arch towered above the local green where he used to play with his mates. Now when he returns to the stadium it's to play for England and tens of thousands cheer him on.

Sterling was five when he arrived in London from Jamaica, the country where he was born. He never knew his dad, who had been murdered when Sterling was two. He lived in London near Wembley with his older sister and their mum. Sterling was always up at 5 a.m. – but not to practise football. His mum worked as a cleaner in a hotel to help pay for her degree, and Sterling helped her clean toilets and change bed sheets before he went to school.

"ENGLAND IS STILL A PLACE WHERE A NAUGHTY BOY WHO COMES FROM NOTHING CAN LIVE HIS DREAM."
Raheem Sterling

Sterling found it hard to concentrate at school, as he couldn't keep still. His life changed when he discovered Sunday League football. It gave him a focus for his energy and he became obsessed by the game. By the time he was ten, he was being scouted by London's top clubs, including Arsenal.

His mum, who Sterling says is the most important figure in his life, advised him to turn Arsenal down. She said it would be better for him to go to a smaller club, where the pressure would be less and he could work his way up. And so, aged ten, he joined Queens Park Rangers.

But QPR trained miles from Sterling's home at Wembley, which meant much of his day was spent on travel: he left school at 3.15 p.m. every weekday to take three buses to get there in time. He only got back home at 11p.m. Since his mum didn't want him travelling on his own and she was at work, his sister accompanied him every single time. Sterling sees his success as a team effort as without his family he never would have made it.

When Sterling was fourteen, he was called up for England's Under-16s and, aged fifteen, he joined Liverpool's Academy. He was homesick in Liverpool, but the club helped him feel at home by arranging for him to live with a couple in their 70s near Anfield, who loved him as if he was their grandson. He made his senior team debut, aged 17 and 107 days, the third youngest player ever to play for the club.

At Liverpool, he played in a variety of positions, including centre-forward, number ten, wing-back and on both wings. He excelled out wide, where his speed and dribbling skills were a nightmare for defenders. He was seventeen when he got his first full England call-up.

After three years at Liverpool he moved to Manchester City for £49 million, the highest amount any club has ever paid for an English player. At City, coach Pep Guardiola improved his game and added finishing to his skill set. Sterling helped City win the 2018 Premier League title by scoring a career-best 23 goals. England also benefited from Sterling's sterling qualities. He was a key starter in the England team that reached the 2018 World Cup semi-final.

Sterling, who has won praise for calling out racism, has never forgotten the sacrifices his family made for his career: his mother struggled to make ends meet and his sister took him to training for years. The love of his family means more than scoring goals. "The day that I bought my mum a house," he said, "that was probably the happiest I've ever been."

STAR PLAYER

WALTER TULL

Spurs star and war hero who challenged the racism of his era

STAR STAT

29

age of death in the First World War

Born: 1888
Died: 1918
Country: England
Position: Midfielder
Major clubs: Tottenham Hotspur (England)

Key | = leader | = innovator | = scorer | = stopper

Walter Tull was a hero three times over: on the pitch, on the battlefield and in life. He was a gifted footballer and a highly regarded army officer. He was also one of the first Britons with black heritage to succeed in these professions at a time when racism and prejudice was rife across society.

Tull's father was born in Barbados and he came to England after working as a ship's carpenter. Tull's mother was from Kent. Tragically both parents died when Tull was a child and, aged nine, he was sent to live in an orphanage. His teachers indulged his passion for football and when Tull was 20 he signed for Clapton, an amateur side in London. In his first season, the club won three trophies including the FA Amateur Cup.

Tull was snapped up by Tottenham Hotspur, who were in the First Division, making him one of the first people of mixed heritage to play professionally in the UK. But he faced terrible prejudice and discrimination, including racist chanting. For example, when Spurs played Bristol City, a newspaper reported that a section of the crowd shouted abuse at Tull. The article said: "Let me tell those Bristol hooligans that Tull is so clean in mind and method as to be a model for all white men who play football."

After two years at Spurs, Tull transferred to Northampton Town. He appeared 111 times until, in 1914, the First World War broke out between Britain and Germany. Within months, Tull had enlisted in the army and was sent to fight. He rose up the ranks to become a second lieutenant. He was one of the first people of black heritage to join the officer class in the regular British Army, at a time when regulations made this almost impossible.

The First World War was fought in many countries and in 1917, when Tull was serving in Italy, he led 26 men on a night raid against an enemy position. All his men returned unharmed despite coming under heavy fire. His seniors commended him for his "gallantry and coolness".

In March 1918, a few months before the end of the war, Tull was stationed in northern France. Germany unleashed a fierce attack on the British front line, firing more than 3.5 million shells. The casualties were horrific: Tull was one of about half a million soldiers who died. He was 29 years old.

On the pitch, Tull had shown great courage in getting on with his job when faced with racist abuse, and even greater bravery with his men during the war. He was one of the first people to begin the fight against racial prejudice in football. On the 100th anniversary of his death, politicians supported a campaign for Tull to be awarded the Military Cross for his exceptional wartime effort.

STAR PLAYER

GEORGE WEAH

King who became President

Born: 1966
Country: Liberia
Position: Centre-forward
Major clubs: Monaco, Paris Saint-Germain (both France), AC Milan (Italy), Chelsea, Manchester City (both England)
International highlights: Played in 1996 Africa Cup of Nations; scored in 2002 Africa Cup of Nations
Individual awards: Winner, 1995 Ballon D'Or

STAR STAT

62%
vote share in Liberia's presidential election

Key | = leader | = innovator | = scorer | = stopper

Fast, powerful, creative and technically brilliant, George Weah is the only African to have won the Ballon D'Or award for the best footballer in the world. Born in Liberia, the centre-forward – nicknamed King George – had a glittering career at European clubs including Paris Saint-Germain and AC Milan, where he scored goals of such breathtaking skill they are still remembered today.

Weah was raised by his grandmother in Monrovia, the capital of Liberia. The West African country is about the same size as Scotland, with roughly the same population. Weah, who has thirteen brothers and sisters, grew up in poverty. When he started playing football, he still had to work as a telephone technician to earn money. His life changed when a French coach in Liberia spotted him and recommended him to Monaco coach Arsène Wenger, who signed him up.

Weah played for four years at Monaco, where he quickly developed into one of the most devastating attackers in European football. He was a prolific goal-scorer with supreme technical skills and explosive acceleration.

In more than a decade in Europe he became known for spectacular goals, most famously one for AC Milan against Verona, when he took the ball in his own penalty area and dribbled past most of the opposite team the length of the pitch before beating the keeper.

Yet Weah's stellar playing career was just the first part of an extraordinary life story. While he was turning into one of the best paid and most famous footballers in the world, Liberia was entering one of the darkest periods in its history. Groups inside the country started to fight each other. The civil war claimed about 250,000 lives and devastated the national economy. Weah, Liberia's greatest national hero, maintained his links with his country during this time. He not only played for the national team, but funded it. He paid for the kit and bought the plane tickets so the team could play away matches.

After retiring from the professional game, Weah returned home. In 2005, he campaigned to become the president of Liberia. He lost the election because his opponents said he was unqualified for the job because he hadn't gone to school. But rather than give up, Weah went and got an education.

“EVERYTHING I DO IN MY LIFE IS TO BENEFIT MY PEOPLE.”
George Weah

He moved to the USA, went to university to study Business Management, and returned to Liberia to try his luck again. In 2014, he was elected as a senator in the Liberian parliament and decided to stand in the presidential elections of 2017. Second time lucky!

In 2018, thousands of Liberians came to see him officially take up his position as president. The ceremony was held in … Monrovia's main football stadium. Even fifteen years into retirement, King George could still pack out the stands. Mr President, what a goal!

STAR PLAYER

LEV YASHIN

Innovative Russian who was the first modern goalkeeper

Born: 1929
Died: 1990
Country: Soviet Union (now Russia)
Position: Goalkeeper
Major clubs: Dynamo Moscow (Soviet Union)
International Highlights: Winner, 1960 Euros; finalist, 1964 Euros; semi-finalist, 1966 World Cup
Individual Awards: Winner, 1963 Ballon D'Or

STAR STAT

74 appearances for the USSR

Key | = leader | = innovator | = scorer | = stopper

Lev Yashin is the only goalkeeper to win the Ballon D'Or, the most prestigious individual award in football. Yet his greatest legacy is that, more than anyone else of his era, he changed the role of his position. Before him, the keeper was largely static and would stand between the posts and wait for attacks to come. Yashin, on the other hand, was dynamic in the box: shouting encouragement to team-mates, organising the defence, running at oncoming attacking players and starting attacks with quick throws and passes. He was also one of the first keepers to punch away crosses rather than always attempt a catch.

Yashin was instantly recognisable. He liked to wear a cloth cap and a dark strip and was given the nickname the Black Spider. No, he didn't crawl around and bite people, nor did he hang from the crossbar on a line of silk. It was because he saved so well, as if he had eight arms and legs! (His home fans called him the Black Panther because of his athleticism.) Funnily enough, his shirt was never black, just very dark blue. Dark Blue Spider doesn't sound as fearsome!

The Union of Soviet Socialist Republics (USSR), or the Soviet Union, existed from 1922 to 1991 and was made up of 15 countries including Russia, Ukraine, Belarus, Latvia, Lithuania, Kazakhstan and Georgia.

Yashin was born in 1929 in Moscow, Russia, which at that time was part of the Soviet Union. During the Second World War, the factory where his dad worked was relocated to a town 500 miles away, so the family moved there too. Yashin started working in the factory at the age of thirteen, but he worked so hard that by the time he was eighteen he was suffering from depression. He managed to get better by joining the army, where he rediscovered his love of sport by playing for a military team. Within a few years he was spotted by a Dynamo Moscow youth coach. As well as being a brilliant football keeper, Yashin also played as a keeper in ice hockey, winning the 1953 Soviet Union Cup.

In 1954, he was called up for the Soviet Union national football team. His composure, positioning and reflex-saves gave him a huge presence in goal, a crucial factor in the Soviet Union's most successful decade. The team won gold medal at the 1956 Olympics, they were champions of the first ever Euros in 1960 and reached the semi-finals of the 1966 World Cup.

Yashin is literally the poster boy of Russian football. He was on FIFA's official poster for the 2018 World Cup.

Among Yashin's personal achievements were 270 clean sheets and 150 penalty-kick saves, more than any other keeper.

One of his greatest moments was also tinged with sadness. After the final whistle of the 1960 Euros – still the only time Russia has won it – fans invaded the pitch. In the chaos, Yashin lost his beloved cloth cap. He never wore a cap again.

Hats off to one of the greatest keepers of all time!

STAR PLAYER

ZINÉDINE ZIDANE

One of the world's greatest players who became one of the best coaches

Born: 1972
Country: France
Position: Midfielder
Major clubs: Juventus (Italy), Real Madrid (Spain)
International highlights (as player): Winner, 1998 World Cup (scored in final); winner, 2000 Euros
International highlights (as coach): Winner, 2016, 2017, 2018 Champions League

STAR STAT

3
goals scored in World Cup finals

Key | = leader | = innovator | = scorer | = stopper

Zinédine Zidane disproves the theory that great players cannot become great coaches. The French midfielder scored in two World Cup finals and 20 years later made history as a coach by guiding Real Madrid to three Champions League triumphs in a row.

Zidane grew up in the port city of Marseille in the south of France. His parents, Malika and Smaïl, were Algerian immigrants and he was the youngest of five children. They lived in a tower block on a housing estate and when he wasn't play fighting with his brother Djamel, he was practising in the local square.

Zidane was an elegant midfielder who seemed to glide across the pitch. He helped his first club, Cannes, qualify for Europe, reached a European final with Bordeaux and won two league titles with Juventus. He then moved to Real Madrid, where he won one league title and the 2002 Champions League thanks to his winning goal, a dramatic dipping volley from outside the area. After the game, he said he wanted to help Real Madrid win the competition three more times.

Today's Special – Only €78 million!

Club president Florentino Pérez asked Zidane to play for Real Madrid by writing a note on a napkin in a restaurant in Monaco. Pérez had to pay Juventus €78 million to sign the Frenchman. What an expensive lunch!

But it was on the biggest stage of all that Zidane gave his most memorable performances. His legacy was sealed when France beat Brazil 3–0 in the 1998 World Cup final. Zidane scored two headers from corners. After the game, crowds on the streets of Paris chanted "Zi-dane Président!"

"THERE IS NO SECRET – JUST A LOT OF HARD WORK."
Zinédine Zidane

Zidane's last ever match was another World Cup final, this time in 2006. In extra time, he headbutted Italy defender Marco Materazzi in the chest and was immediately sent off. France lost but no one blamed Zidane. Materazzi had supposedly been rude about Zidane's sister, and Zidane was defending his family's honour. The incident has become a famous part of French football history and a statue, called *Le Headbutt*, stood proudly outside one of the country's most famous museums, the Pompidou Centre.

Zidane stepped away from the spotlight before returning to Real Madrid. He worked as advisor to club president Florentino Pérez, and also as assistant coach and B team coach, before he was named head coach in January 2016. As Real Madrid coach, he guided the team to three consecutive Champions League titles: 2016, 2017 and 2018. No other coach has come close to this achievement, and he had finally fulfilled that dream he'd had back in 2002.

As a player, Zidane was famous for his sense of the collective, always bringing out the best in his team-mates. The same was true as a coach. Zidane understood what his players needed. He encouraged and protected them. He didn't speak much but when he did, everyone listened.

He shocked Real Madrid when he quit in 2018. No coach chooses to leave Real Madrid: normally they wait until they are sacked! But Zidane has always been different. He is a winner: both as a player and as a coach. Although he had weaknesses – his short temper among them – he remained humble and hardworking. When Zidane quit as coach, Florentino Pérez said it was a sad day. "It's not for me," Zidane replied. Once again, Zidane had left the stage on his own terms.

FOOTBALL SCHOOL

1. What is Eniola Aluko's favourite book?

a) *Football School*
b) *Paddington*
c) *To Kill a Mockingbird*
d) *Great Expectations*

2. Roberto Baggio was the first person to do what?

a) Cry in a World Cup final
b) Miss the decisive penalty in a World Cup final shoot-out
c) Have the name Roberto and play for Italy
d) Score a hat-trick in a World Cup final

3. Why did a coach claim Gareth Bale was jinxed?

a) He didn't win in his first 24 appearances.
b) He could only score goals with overhead kicks.
c) He had a crazy haircut.
d) He had a pet dragon called Griffin.

4. What World Cup record does Franz Beckenbauer hold?

a) The first defender to score a World Cup hat-trick.
b) The first coach to wear lederhosen at a World Cup.
c) The first man to drink a yard of ale on a World Cup pitch.
d) The first man to win the World Cup as a captain and a coach.

5. What was David Beckham wearing when his picture appeared on the side of a bus?

a) A kilt
b) A sarong
c) His underpants
d) Manchester City kit

STAR PLAYERS QUIZ

6. What job did Lucy Bronze dream of having when she grew up?

a) Accountant
b) Astronaut
c) Chef
d) Footballer

7. What record does Brazilian goalkeeper Rogério Ceni hold?

a) Most penalties ever saved
b) Most goals ever scored by a goalkeeper
c) Most red cards ever received
d) Biggest hands ever recorded

8. In 1968, Bobby Charlton became the first Englishman to do what?

a) Captain a winning team in the European Cup
b) Score from the halfway line at Wembley
c) Play for Manchester United and City in the same season
d) Sing "God Save the Queen" at the Royal Albert Hall

9. What part of her body does Brandi Chastain want to donate to scientific research after her death?

a) Feet
b) Knees
c) Heart
d) Brain

10. What have the FA named at the national training centre in honour of David Clarke's influence on blind football in England?

a) An arch
b) A changing room
c) A sandwich shop
d) A fountain

11. What title did Liv Cooke win in 2017?

a) Ballon D'Or
b) European Championship top scorer
c) Freestyle Football World Champion
d) Women's Super League Player of the Year

12. The style of football Johan Cruyff invented in the Netherlands was called:

a) Dutch Football
b) Fantastic Football
c) Total Football
d) Tulip Football

13. Which club did Kenny Dalglish play for before he joined Liverpool?

a) Aberdeen
b) Celtic
c) Everton
d) Rangers

14. What does Didier Deschamps believe is crucial to having a good conversation?

a) All phones should be out of sight.
b) Every word should be whispered.
c) Everyone should use an ear-trumpet.
d) The most important part of the conversation should be sung.

15. In which country did hero Didier Drogba help stop the civil war?

a) Angola
b) Ivory Coast
c) Liberia
d) Rwanda

16. What does Edin Džeko's nickname Bosanski Dijamant mean in English?

a) Bosnian Dalmation
b) Bosnian Diamond
c) Bosnian DJ
d) Bosnian Jam

17. What is a biofuel, the product made by France midfielder Mathieu Flamini's company?

a) A petrol substitute made from plants and trees
b) A protein shake
c) Fart gas
d) Natural yoghurt

18. What has Pep Guardiola admitted to sometimes thinking during games?

a) What's for my tea?
b) Why is it raining again?
c) Do you think the cameras will catch me if I pick my nose?
d) What would Johan Cruyff do?

19. How did Béla Guttmann find out about a rising talent called Eusébio, who would go on to become one of Portugal's best ever players?

a) Eusébio's mother wrote him a letter.
b) Eusébio kicked a ball through Guttmann's kitchen window.
c) Eusébio scored a hat-trick against Guttmann's Benfica in a friendly.
d) Someone at the barber's told him.

20. What disease killed England international Jeff Hall and is now eradicated in the UK?

a) Cholera
b) Measles
c) Polio
d) Tuberculosis

21. How old was American Mia Hamm when she made her international debut?

a) 15
b) 20
c) 25
d) 30

22. Norway's Ada Hegerberg was the first winner of what?

a) Women's Golden Boot
b) Women's Ballon D'Or
c) Women's Golden Reindeer
d) Women's Golden Shoe

23. What piece of sporting kit inspired Craig Johnston to invent a new football boot?

a) Baseball mitt
b) Cricket pad
c) Shuttlecock
d) Table-tennis bat

24. Which team released Harry Kane when he was eight?

a) Arsenal
b) Chelsea
c) Fulham
d) West Ham

25. What rule did former Iran captain Katayoun Khosrowyar persuade FIFA to change?

a) Allowing goalkeepers to use their hands
b) The ban on hijab headscarves
c) Oranges at half-time
d) Using VAR

26. Why is Vincent Kompany's dad famous in Belgium?

a) He is the first black mayor elected in Brussels.
b) He coaches a team called Kompany.
c) He wrote a book about parents of famous children.
d) He won the Tour de France as a cyclist.

27. How many England players did Diego Maradona dribble past to score what was voted Goal of the Century in the 1986 World Cup?

a) 0
b) 3
c) 5
d) 7

28. What country did Marta play in after she left Brazil, winning seven league titles?

a) Argentina
b) England
c) Sweden
d) USA

29. What is the name of the charity Juan Mata set up to help people around the world?

a) Common Goal
b) Offside Goal
c) Own Goal
d) Wonder Goal

30. What sport did Kylian Mbappé's mum, Fayza, play professionally?

a) Basketball
b) Football
c) Handball
d) Snooker

31. How old was Lionel Messi when he left Argentina and moved to Barcelona, who had agreed to pay for his medical treatment?

a) 10
b) 13
c) 16
d) 19

32. What award did Luka Modrić win at the 2018 World Cup?

a) Best goal celebration of the tournament
b) Best headband of the tournament
c) Best penalty of the tournament
d) Best player of the tournament

33. How do Nadia Nadim's family refer to her enthusiasm for life?

a) The Afghan Spirit
b) The Danish Joy
c) The Nadi Effect
d) The Wow-Amazing-Brilliant-Go-For-It-Mindset

34. What is the name for a new type of goalkeeping invented by Manuel Neuer, in which goalies often play outside their area?

a) Handy-Manny
b) Helicopter defending
c) Holy goalie
d) Sweeper-keeper

35. What was the nickname of the hairstyle Neymar revealed at the 2018 World Cup?

a) Spaghetti curls
b) Hot-dog mullet
c) Top-knot turkey
d) Mohawk madness

36. Where did Lily Parr's club, Dick, Kerr's Ladies, get its name from?

a) Brenda Dick and Janet Kerr founded the team.
b) Dick and Kerr are towns in Lancashire.
c) Dick, Kerr was a factory the players worked at.
d) The players' favourite meal was spotted dick, and the fans chanted "Kerr-ching!" because they won so often.

37. Which inventor was Pelé named after?

a) Alexander Graham Bell
b) Thomas Edison
c) Nikola Tesla
d) The Wright brothers

38. What nickname was Ferenc Puskás known by due to the army connections with his Hungarian club Honvéd?

a) The Corpulent Corporal
b) The Galloping Major
c) The Scoring Sergeant
d) The Offside Officer

39. Who does USA Star Player Megan Rapinoe run her fashion label with?

a) Her girlfriend Sue Bird
b) Her head coach Jill Ellis
c) Her team-mate Alex Morgan
d) Her twin sister Rachael

40. What job did Cyrille Regis have before he became a West Brom and England star?

a) Doctor
b) Electrician
c) Inventor
d) Salesman

41. Why did Rose Reilly move to France to play football?

a) Her favourite breakfast was croissants.
b) She wanted to learn French.
c) She was fed up with cold Scottish winters.
d) The FA had banned women from playing at major grounds.

42. Why did Jules Rimet invent the World Cup?

a) His dad owned a trophy shop.
b) He wanted to bring nations together peacefully.
c) He wanted something to look forward to in the summer.
d) He wanted France to win something.

43. What was the nickname given to Brazil's strike-force of Ronaldo, Rivaldo and Ronaldinho, that won the 2002 World Cup?

a) The Three Rs
b) The two Ronnies and the Rivi
c) RoRiRo
d) Ronivaldozinho

44. For which national team did transgender defender Jaiyah Saelua play in a World Cup qualifier?

a) American Samoa
b) Fiji
c) Bahamas
d) Tonga

45. What message did Mo Salah's dad give that Salah said changed his life?

a) Be nice and keep smiling
b) Brush your hair and pull up your socks
c) Keep going and train hard
d) Run faster and score more

46. What London landmark could Raheem Sterling see from his childhood home?

a) Big Ben
b) Madame Tussauds
c) The Shard
d) Wembley Stadium

47. What was war hero and former Spurs player Walter Tull praised for during his time in the army?

a) His cooking and joke-telling
b) His gallantry and coolness
c) His keepy-uppies
d) His singing

48. In 1995 George Weah became the first African to do what?

a) Win the Ballon D'Or
b) Become president of Liberia
c) Play for Paris Saint-Germain
d) Score a European Cup final hat-trick

49. Lev Yashin was known as the Black Spider internationally, but what did Russians call him?

a) The Black Bat
b) The Black Cat
c) The Black Caviar
d) The Black Panther

50. How did Real Madrid president Florentino Pérez ask Zinédine Zidane to sign for his club?

a) He sent him a dozen red roses.
b) He wrote a note on a napkin in a restaurant they were both at.
c) He dressed up as Napoleon Bonaparte and asked if he wanted to move to Madrid.
d) He hid his Real Madrid contract in a bowl of spaghetti.

FOOTBALL SCHOOL

1. **Aluko**
   c)
2. **Baggio**
   b)
3. **Bale**
   a)
4. **Beckenbauer**
   d)
5. **Beckham**
   c)
6. **Bronze**
   a)
7. **Ceni**
   b)
8. **Charlton**
   a)
9. **Chastain**
   d)
10. **Clarke**
    b)
11. **Cooke**
    c)
12. **Cruyff**
    c)
13. **Dalglish**
    b)
14. **Deschamps**
    a)
15. **Drogba**
    b)
16. **Džeko**
    b)
17. **Flamini**
    a)
18. **Guardiola**
    d)
19. **Guttmann**
    d)
20. **Hall**
    c)
21. **Hamm**
    a)
22. **Hegerberg**
    b)
23. **Johnston**
    d)
24. **Kane**
    a)

STAR PLAYERS QUIZ ANSWERS

25. **Khosrowyar**
    b)
26. **Kompany**
    a)
27. **Maradona**
    c)
28. **Marta**
    c)
29. **Mata**
    a)
30. **Mbappé**
    c)
31. **Messi**
    b)
32. **Modrić**
    d)
33. **Nadim**
    c)
34. **Neuer**
    d)
35. **Neymar**
    a)
36. **Parr**
    c)
37. **Pelé**
    b)
38. **Puskás**
    b)
39. **Rapinoe**
    d)
40. **Regis**
    b)
41. **Reilly**
    d)
42. **Rimet**
    b)
43. **Ronaldo**
    a)
44. **Saelua**
    a)
45. **Salah**
    c)
46. **Sterling**
    d)
47. **Tull**
    b)
48. **Weah**
    a)
49. **Yashin**
    d)
50. **Zidane**
    b)

FOOTBALL SCHOOL

JANUARY

2 Nadia Nadim
2 Rose Reilly
18 Pep Guardiola
22 Rogério Ceni
27 Béla Guttmann

FEBRUARY

5 Neymar
9 Cyrille Regis
18 Roberto Baggio
19 Marta
21 Eniola Aluko

MARCH

4 Kenny Dalglish
7 Mathieu Flamini
11 Didier Drogba
17 Edin Džeko
17 Mia Hamm
27 Manuel Neuer

APRIL

2 Ferenc Puskás
10 Vincent Kompany
20 Liv Cooke
25 Johan Cruyff
26 Lily Parr
28 Juan Mata
28 Walter Tull

MAY

2 David Beckham

JUNE

15 Mo Salah
23 Zinédine Zidane
24 Lionel Messi
25 Craig Johnston

STAR PLAYERS BIRTHDAY CALENDAR

JULY

5 Megan Rapinoe
10 Ada Hegerberg
16 Gareth Bale
19 Jaiyah Saelua
21 Brandi Chastain
28 Harry Kane

AUGUST

SEPTEMBER

7 Jeff Hall
9 Luka Modrić
11 Franz Beckenbauer
11 David Clarke
19 Katayoun Khosrowyar
22 Ronaldo

OCTOBER

1 George Weah
11 Bobby Charlton
14 Jules Rimet
15 Didier Deschamps
22 Lev Yashin
23 Pelé
28 Lucy Bronze
30 Diego Maradona

NOVEMBER

No presents to buy this month!

DECEMBER

8 Raheem Sterling
20 Kylian Mbappé

FOOTBALL SCHOOL

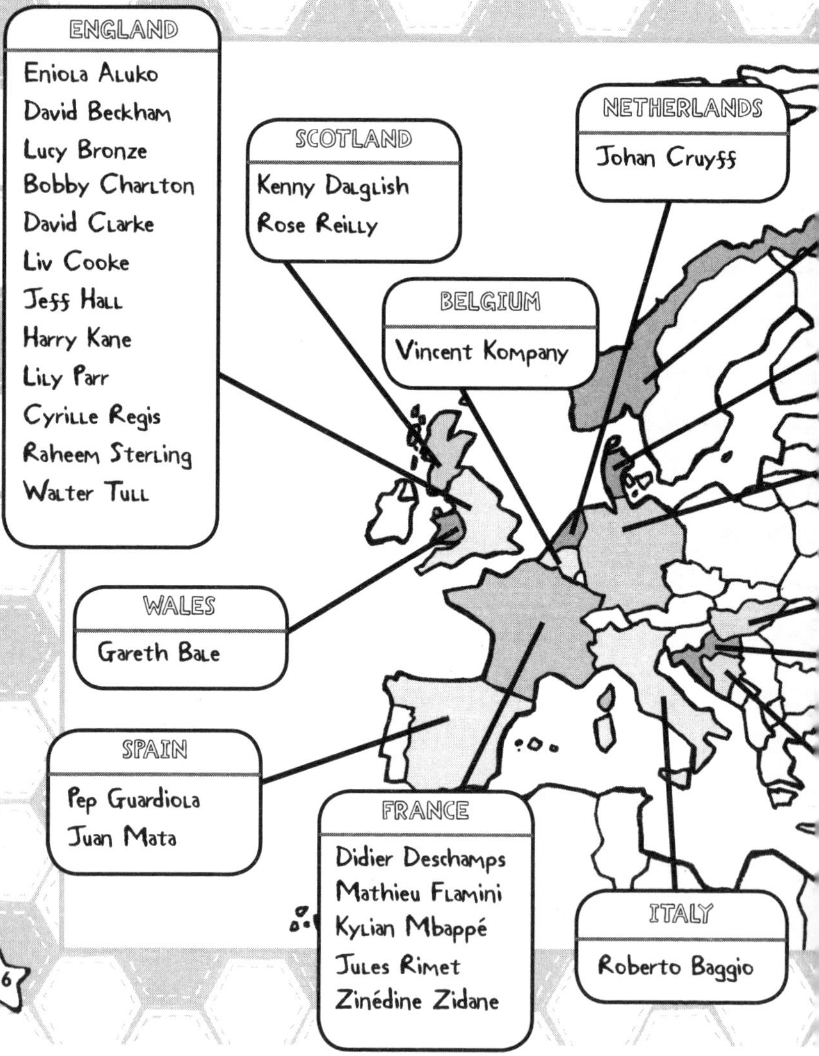

STAR PLAYERS IN EUROPE

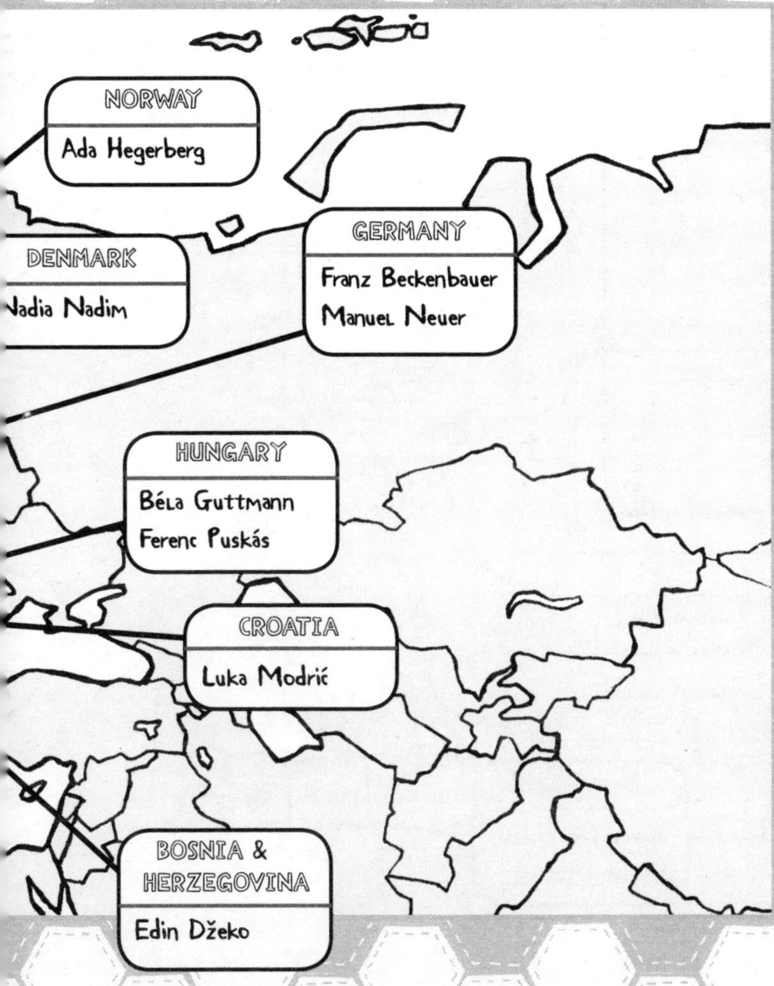

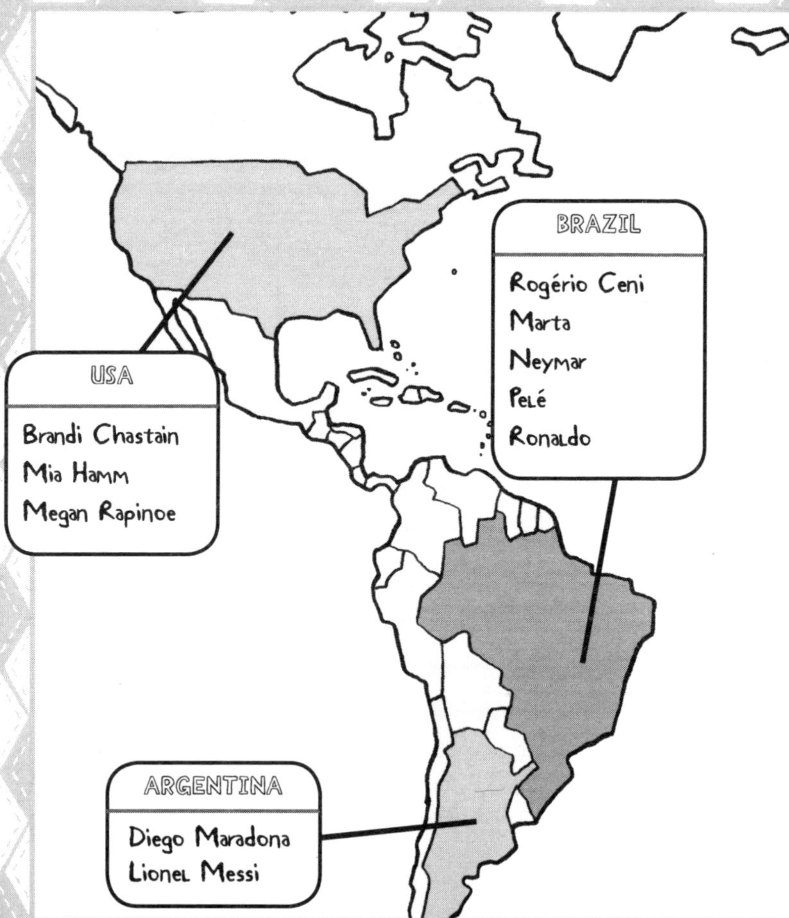
USA
Brandi Chastain
Mia Hamm
Megan Rapinoe
BRAZIL
Rogério Ceni
Marta
Neymar
Pelé
Ronaldo
ARGENTINA
Diego Maradona
Lionel Messi

STAR PLAYERS IN THE REST OF THE WORLD

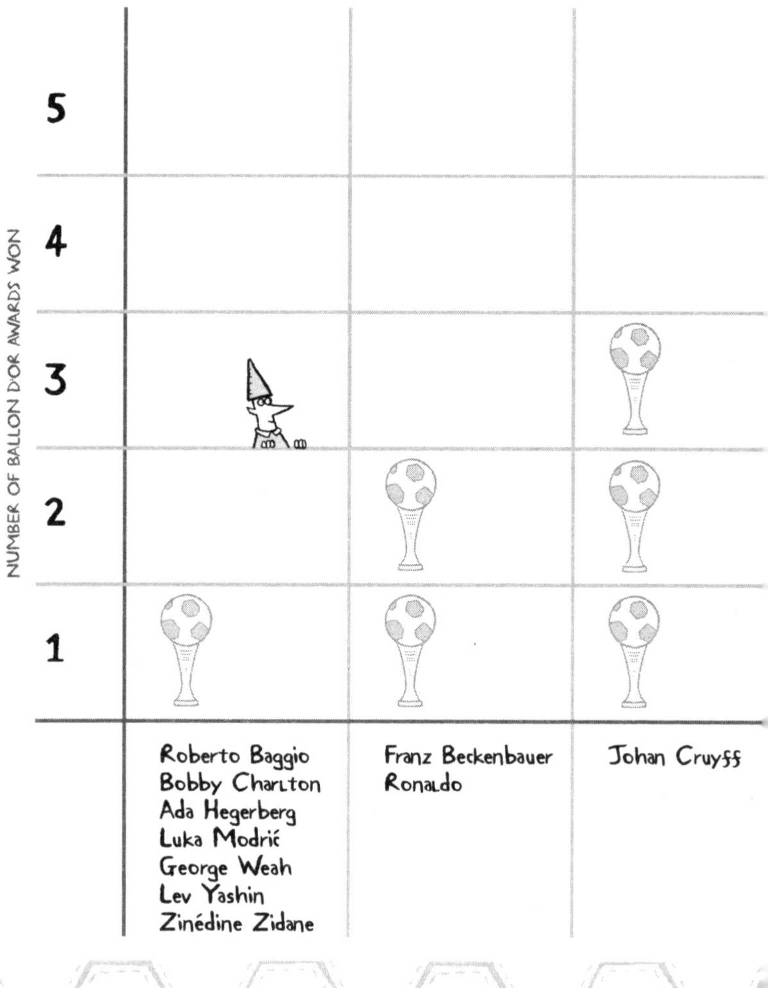
NUMBER OF BALLON D'OR AWARDS WON
5
4
3
2
1
Roberto Baggio
Bobby Charlton
Ada Hegerberg
Luka Modrić
George Weah
Lev Yashin
Zinédine Zidane
Franz Beckenbauer
Ronaldo
Johan Cruyff

WINNERS OF THE BALLON D'OR

	Lionel Messi	

FOOTBALL SCHOOL

Football School

Kickito Ergo Sum

STAR PLAYER

Born: ....

Country: ....

Position: ....

Major clubs: ....

International highlights: ....

....

Individual awards: ....

....

STAR STAT

DRAW YOUR HEROES

STAR PLAYER

Born: ....

Country: ....

Position: ....

Major clubs: ....

International highlights: ....

....

Individual awards: ....

....

STAR STAT

That's all, folks! We started with Aluko and finished with Zidane.
She is aaamazing and he is ... zzzuperb!
Hang on. Zuperb isn't a word?
It iz now!!!
We've had a blast telling you about the world's best footballers.
The superstars whose talent has lit up the game over the last hundred years.
We've debated who is the best ever: Pelé or Maradona? Marta or Mia Hamm?
Alex or Ben?

Hmmm... Surely Spike, who drew all the pictures!
We've been awed by people with stories of incredible resilience, determination and bravery. Like Nadia Nadim, who fled Afghanistan to become a scoring sensation.
And Edin Džeko, who survived a war to take his country to the World Cup for the first time.
Whoops, I realise we've forgotten someone!
This person is currently alive, has a brilliant sense of humour and a great future ahead of them.
Yes, YOU. The person reading these words now.
Hurrah for our Star Readers! Zee you all zzzooon!

ACKNOWLEDGEMENTS

It may have been hard to select the 50 outstanding players for this book but there is no question who our Star Illustrator is. Spike Gerrell is our creative crayon conqueror whose images have brought these Star Players to life. Super, Spike!

The team at Walker always bring out the best in us: head coach Daisy Jellicoe, creative playmaker Laurelie Bazin and sporting director Denise Johnstone-Burt. Thanks also to Louise Jackson, Rosi Crawley, Megan Middleton, James McParland, Ed Ripley, Jill Kidson, John Moore, Jamie Hammond and Jo Humphreys-Davies. New signing Rebecca Oram is a fantastic addition to the team!

Our star agents Rebecca Carter, Kirsty Gordon, Ellis Hazelgrove, David Luxton, Rebecca Winfield and Nick Walters provided us with top backroom support.

We would also like to thank the following, some of whom helped arrange interviews with the Star Players, for their time and expertise: Mercedes Antrobus, Jeff Davis, Sam Jackson, Behrman Jafarzadeh, Michael Kallback, Danny Lynch, Ben Miller, James Montague, Will Smith, Jo Tongue, Darren Tulett, Grant Wahl, whose excellent book *Football 2.0* is highly recommended, Jonathan Wilson and Dan Wood.

A shout-out to our Star Pupils Oscar Auerbach, Christiana and Nicholas Burt, Billy Cooke, Sammy Kain, Iolo Madryn Rhys and Ivo Prosser. Thank you also to Arthur Bullard, the Star Player at Spike's studio.

Ben would like to thank Annie for her continual inspiration and support of Football School all over the country, and Clemmy and Bibi for being Football School's funnest fans. You are the best!

Alex would like to thank Nat, Zak and Barnaby.

ABOUT YOUR COACHES

Alex Bellos writes for the *Guardian*. He has written several bestselling popular science books and created two mathematical colouring books. He loves puzzles.

Ben Lyttleton is a journalist, broadcaster and football consultant. He has written books about how to score the perfect penalty and what we can learn from football's best managers.

Spike Gerrell grew up loving both playing football and drawing pictures. He now gets to draw for a living. At heart, though, he will always be a central midfielder.

FOOTBALL SCHOOL
SEASON 1
WHERE FOOTBALL EXPLAINS THE WORLD
Rules
FOOTBALL SCHOOL
SEASON 2
WHERE FOOTBALL EXPLAINS THE WORLD
Saves
Alex Bellos
Ben Lyttleton
COLLECT THE FOOTBALL SCHOOL SERIES
FOOTBALL SCHOOL
SEASON 3
WHERE FOOTBALL EXPLAINS THE WORLD
tackles
Alex Bellos
Ben Lyttleton
OVER 300 FAN-TASTIC QUESTIONS
FOOTBALL SCHOOL
THE AMAZING QUIZ BOOK
TEST YOUR WORLD CUP KNOWLEDGE!
Alex Bellos
Ben Lyttleton
FOOTBALL SCHOOL
SEASON 4
WHERE FOOTBALL EXPLAINS THE WORLD
Celebrates
Alex Bellos
Ben Lyttleton